Houghton Mifflin

California Math

Homework and Problem Solving

Student Book

- Homework
- Leveled Problem Solving

GRADE 2

 HOUGHTON MIFFLIN   BOSTON

Printed in the U.S.A.

ISBN 10: 0-618-96127-5
ISBN 13: 978-0-618-96127-6

16 17 18 19 0982 16 15 14 13
4500413910

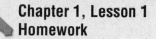
Hands On: Make Ten to Add

CA Standards
KEY NS 2.2, MR 1.2

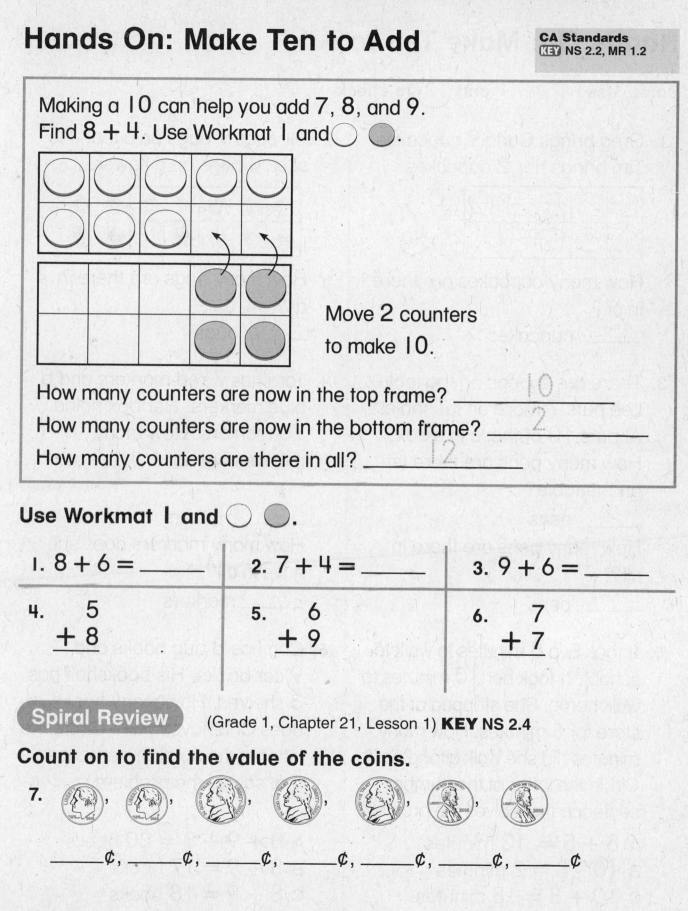

Making a 10 can help you add 7, 8, and 9.
Find 8 + 4. Use Workmat 1 and ◯ ●.

Move 2 counters
to make 10.

How many counters are now in the top frame? _____ 10

How many counters are now in the bottom frame? _____ 2

How many counters are there in all? _____ 12

Use Workmat 1 and ◯ ●.

1. 8 + 6 = _____	2. 7 + 4 = _____	3. 9 + 6 = _____

4. 5
   + 8
	5. 6
	   + 9
		6. 7
		   + 7

Spiral Review   (Grade 1, Chapter 21, Lesson 1) **KEY** NS 2.4

Count on to find the value of the coins.

7. ◯, ◯, ◯, ◯, ◯, ◯, ◯

_____¢, _____¢, _____¢, _____¢, _____¢, _____¢, _____¢

Name _____ Date _____

Hands On: Make Ten to Add

CA Standards
KEY NS 2.2, MR 1.2

Solve. Use [grid] and ◯ to check.

1. Greg brings Carla 9 cupcakes. Tim brings her 2 cupcakes.

How many cupcakes are there in all?

_____ cupcakes

2. Bill sees 9 bugs on a leaf. He sees 4 bugs on a flower.

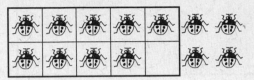

How many bugs are there in all?

_____ bugs

3. There are 6 pens on the table. Lee puts 7 more on the table. Al puts 10 of these in a box. How many pens are there left on the table?

_____ pens

How many pens are there in all?

_____ pens

4. Tara has 7 red markers and 5 blue markers. Her box holds 10 markers. How many markers will not fit in the box?

_____ markers

How many markers does she have in all?

_____ markers

5. It took Eva 8 minutes to walk to school. It took her 10 minutes to walk home. She stopped at the store for 5 minutes. How many minutes did she walk altogether? Circle the letter of the number sentence that solves the problem.

A $8 + 5 = 13$ minutes

B $10 - 8 = 2$ minutes

C $10 + 8 = 18$ minutes

6. Chu has 8 bug books and 9 car books. His bookshelf has 3 shelves. How many books does Chu have in all? Circle the letter of the number sentence that solves the problem.

A $8 + 9 + 3 = 20$ books

B $8 + 9 = 17$ books

C $8 + 9 = 18$ books

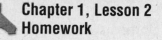
Add Three Numbers

CA Standards
KEY AF 1.1, AF 1.0

Add three numbers. First see if you can make 10 with two numbers.

$$\begin{array}{r} 4 \\ 1 \longrightarrow 10 \\ +9 \end{array} \qquad \begin{array}{r} 4 \\ +10 \\ \hline 14 \end{array}$$

Add three numbers. First add two numbers. Then add the third number.

$$\begin{array}{r} 6 \\ 5 \longrightarrow 11 \\ +2 \end{array} \qquad \begin{array}{r} 11 \\ +2 \\ \hline 13 \end{array}$$

Find the sum. Look for two numbers to add first.

1. $\begin{array}{r} 8 \\ 2 \\ +5 \\ \hline \end{array}$	2. $\begin{array}{r} 6 \\ 4 \\ +1 \\ \hline \end{array}$	3. $\begin{array}{r} 5 \\ 5 \\ +3 \\ \hline \end{array}$
4. $\begin{array}{r} 5 \\ 7 \\ +6 \\ \hline \end{array}$	5. $\begin{array}{r} 4 \\ 9 \\ +2 \\ \hline \end{array}$	6. $\begin{array}{r} 7 \\ 4 \\ +0 \\ \hline \end{array}$

Spiral Review   (Grade 1, Chapter 21, Lesson 2) **NS 1.5**

Draw 2 ways to show each amount.

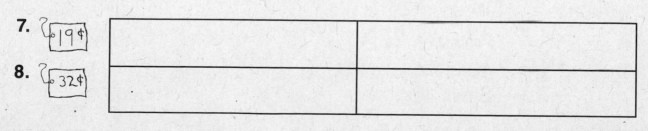

7. 19¢

8. 32¢

Name _____ Date _____

Add Three Numbers

CA Standards
KEY AF 1.1, AF 1.0

Solve.

1. There are 3 robins, 7 bluebirds, and 5 sparrows in a tree. How many birds are in the tree? [Hint: add 7 and 3 first to make 10.]

   _____ birds

2. There are 8 balls and 2 blocks in a toy chest. Mary puts 7 dolls in the chest. How many toys are in the chest? [Hint: add 8 and 2 first to make 10.]

   _____ toys

3. Bud gathers 7 golf balls, 3 Ping-Pong balls, and 7 tennis balls. How many balls does Bud gather?

   _____ balls

4. Mike helps the teacher by collecting 3 books, 4 erasers, and 6 rulers. How many items does Mike collect?

   _____ items

5. Stan uses 3 colors of paper for a project. He uses 6 pieces of red paper, 5 pieces of yellow paper, and 6 pieces of blue paper. How many pieces of paper does he use in all?

   _____ pieces of paper

6. Mary eats 3 apples, 8 oranges, 5 carrots, and 4 peaches. How many pieces of fruit does she eat altogether?

   _____ pieces

Hands On: Fact Familes

CA Standards
KEY NS 2.1, MR 3.0

A fact family is a set of related facts.
Fact familes can help you add and subtract.

Complete the number sentences.

$6 + 7 = \underline{13}$ $7 + 6 = \underline{13}$ $13 - 6 = \underline{7}$ $13 - 7 = \underline{6}$

Complete the number sentences for each fact family.

1. $\underline{} + 5 = 11$

   $\underline{} + 6 = 11$

   $11 - \underline{} = 5$

   $11 - 5 = \underline{}$

2. $3 + 4 = \underline{}$

   $4 + \underline{} = 7$

   $7 - \underline{} = 4$

   $7 - 4 = \underline{}$

3. $8 + 2 = \underline{}$

   $2 + \underline{} = 10$

   $10 - \underline{} = 8$

   $10 - \underline{} = 2$

4. $\underline{} + 3 = 13$

   $\underline{} + 10 = 13$

   $13 - \underline{} = 3$

   $13 - \underline{} = 10$

Spiral Review   (Grade 1, Chapter 21, Lesson 3) **NS 1.5**

Circle the coins that match the price.

5. 42¢

Hands On: Fact Families

CA Standards
KEY NS 2.1, MR 3.0

Add or subtract to solve. Think about fact families.

1. Laura has 8 daisy stickers. She also has 6 rose stickers. How many stickers does she have in all?

   _____ stickers

2. Lee has 6 pets in all. He gives 2 fish to his aunt. How many pets does he have left?

   _____ pets

3. Carl lights 5 blue candles and 6 red candles. How many candles does Carl light in all?

   _____ candles

   The wind blew out 5 of the candles. How many candles are still lit?

   _____ candles

4. Sarah places 3 striped pillows and 4 solid pillows on her bed. How many pillows does she have in all?

   _____ pillows

   Sarah removes the solid pillows. How many pillows are still on her bed?

   _____ pillows

5. Jim has 18 marbles in all. His favorite marbles are the 9 blue ones. Jim trades his marbles that are not blue for 6 sparkle marbles. How many marbles does he have in all?

   _____ marbles

6. Jan packs 8 sandwiches and 7 apples, and 8 containers of juice. Then she unpacks all of the apples. How many food items does Jan pack?

   _____ items

Use with text pp. 9–10

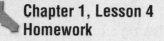
Missing Addends

CA Standard
KEY NS 2.1

Find the missing addend. To find the missing addend, subtract the part from the whole.

____ + 4 = 10

Think 10 − 4 = ____

The missing addend is __6__.

Whole	
10	
Part	**Part**
4	?

Find the missing addend.

1. ____ + 7 = 13

2. 6 + ____ = 15

3. 5 + ____ = 7

4. ____ + 3 = 12

5. ____ + 5 = 10

6. 4 + ____ = 5

7. Shirley has 15 containers of spice in her kitchen. She finishes 7 containers. How many containers does she have left?

_____

Spiral Review   (Grade 1, Chapter 21, Lesson 4) **NS 1.5**

8. There are many different ways to show the same amount. Draw coins to show 35¢ in different ways.

Missing Addends

CA Standard
KEY NS 2.1

Solve the problems using missing addends.

1. Louisa has 6 books on a shelf. She takes 1 book down to read. How many books are left on the shelf?

   _____ books

2. Maria has 7 buttons on her coat. 3 buttons pop off. How many buttons are left on her coat?

   _____ buttons

3. Dan needs 17 comic books to complete his collection. So far he has 9 comic books. How many more comic books does he need?

   _____ comic books

4. Nate sets up 8 chairs for the meeting. 14 people show up. How many more chairs does Nate need to add?

   _____ chairs

5. Sandy cuts 16 pieces of apple pie. She gives away 7 pieces. Then she cuts a peach pie into 8 pieces. How many pieces of apple pie does she have left?

   _____ pieces

6. Carl has 7 square windows on his house. He also has 5 round windows. He places candles in 4 of the square windows. How many windows do not have candles?

   _____ windows

Write a Number Sentence

CA Standards
AF 1.2, MR 2.1

Use a number sentence to solve a problem.

There are 6 rabbits in the garden.
5 more rabbits hop into the garden.
How many rabbits are in the garden in all?

$6 + 5 =$ _____

Write a number sentence to solve.

1. There are 12 squirrels in the tree.
   7 squirrels jump down. How many
   squirrels are left in the tree?

   ____ − ____ = _____ squirrels

2. Chris brings 6 cans for recycling.
   Rikki brings 9 cans. How many
   cans did they bring in all?

   ____ + ____ = _____ cans

3. 8 birds are sitting on the fence.
   4 birds fly away. How many
   birds are left on the fence?

   ____ − ____ = _____ birds

Spiral Review (Grade 1, Chapter 21, Lesson 4) **NS 1.5**

4. There are many different ways to show the same amount. Draw coins
   to show 52¢ in different ways.

Name _____ Date _____

Write a Number Sentence

CA Standard
AF 1.2, MR 2.1

Solve.

1. Bob has 14 toy cars. He gives 7 of his cars to his baby brother. How many toy cars does he have left?

   ____ − ____ = ____ toy cars

2. Shira reads her book for 5 minutes before dinner and 10 minutes after dinner. How many minutes does she spend reading?

   ____ + ____ = ____ minutes

3. The trainer at the aquarium feeds 9 fish to the dolphins. He has 8 fish left. How many fish did he start with?

   ____ ◯ ____ = ____ fish

4. Dan ran 5 miles on Monday. David ran 7 miles more than Dan. How many miles did David run?

   ____ ◯ ____ = ____ miles

5. Becky has 6 toy boxes. 4 toy boxes are filled with toys. She empties out 2 toy boxes. Now how many toy boxes are empty?

   _____ toy boxes

6. Jack has 6 tomato seeds. Stella gives Jack 5 apple seeds. He plants 4 tomato seeds. How many seeds does he have left?

   _____ seeds

Hands On: Make a Tally

CA Standards
KEY SDAP 1.0, SDAP 1.1

Wanda asked her family which fruits they liked best.

Favorite Fruits

Fruit	Tally Marks
apples	I
bananas	III

Which vegetables do your family members like best? Take a survey.

Vegetables	Tally Marks
potatoes	
carrots	
broccoli	

Use data in your chart to answer the questions.

1. How many family members liked potatoes the best?

    _____ family members

2. Which vegetable got the most votes? _____

3. Which vegetable got the least votes? _____

4. Look at the results of the Favorite Fruits survey.
   How many family members voted in all? _____

Spiral Review (Chapter 1, Lesson 1) **KEY NS 2.2**

Make ten to add.

5. $5 + 7 =$ _____   6. $8 + 4 =$ _____   7. $9 + 3 =$ _____

Hands On: Make a Tally

CA Standards
KEY SDAP 1.0, 1.1

1. Bill took a survey of some of his friends to find out which kind of movie they liked best. 6 liked cartoons the best. 4 liked adventure the best. 8 liked mystery the best. Which type of movie was liked the best?

_____

2. Julie asked her friends which types of books they liked the best. 3 liked fairy tales the best. 5 liked history the best. 9 liked mystery the best. Which type of book was liked the least?

_____

3. Tina asks her friends about their favorite game. 4 children like tag best. 3 children like jump rope best. 5 children like hopscotch best. How many friends does Tina ask?

_____

4. Joe asks his friends what their favorite kind of juice is. 3 like apple juice the best. 7 like orange juice the best. 9 like cranberry juice the best. How many friends does Joe ask?

_____

5. Rachel takes a survey of 16 classmates. 4 children like apples best. 7 children like bananas best. The rest of the children like watermelon best. How many tally marks does Rachel make for watermelon?

_____

6. Daniel surveys 19 of his friends for their favorite school subject. English and history each get a score of 5. 2 students like science best. The rest of his friends like math the best. How many tally marks does Daniel make for math?

_____

Compare Data in Tables

CA Standards
KEY SDAP 1.0, AF 1.3

The children in Nina's Class and Edward's class chose their favorite activity.

Nina's Class	
Tennis	|||
Dance		

Edward's Class	
Tennis	₩
Dance	|||

Which class likes Tennis more?

Edward's Class

The children in Stuart's class and Sharon's class choose their favorite accessory.

Stuart's Class	
Hats	₩
Necklace	|||
Scarf	||||

Sharon's Class	
Hats		
Necklace	||
Scarf	₩

1. Which class likes hats more?

_____

2. Which class likes scarves more?

_____

3. How many more students chose necklaces in Stuart's class than Sharon's?

_____

4. How many students voted in Sharon's class?

_____

Spiral Review (Chapter 1 Lesson 2) KEY AF 1.0, KEY AF 1.1

Look for two numbers to add first. Find the Sum.

5. $8 + 2 + 5 =$ _____

6. $7 + 6 + 3 =$ _____

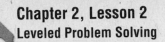
Compare Data in Tables

CA Standard
KEY SDAP 1.0, AF1.3

Shawn asked a **2**nd grade class and a **3**rd grade class to choose the breakfast they liked best.

2nd Grade		3rd Grade	
Oatmeal	7	Oatmeal	3
Eggs	4	Eggs	9
Pancakes	1	Pancakes	3
Cereal	6	Cereal	2

Use both tables to answer the questions.

1. How many 2nd graders like oatmeal best?

_____

2. How many 3rd graders like pancakes best?

_____

3. How many more 3rd graders than 2nd graders like eggs the best?

_____

4. How many more 2nd graders than 3rd graders like oatmeal the best?

_____

5. 3 2nd graders change their minds and decide they like pancakes the best instead of cereal. How many like cereal the best?

_____

How many like pancakes?

_____

6. 3 3rd graders change their minds and decide they like eggs more than pancakes. How many 3rd graders like eggs the best?

_____

How many like pancakes the best?

_____

Name _____ Date _____

Read a Picture Graph

CA Standards
SDAP 1.2, AF 1.3

A picture graph uses symbols to show information.

How many bananas are for sale? __6__

How many apples are for sale? __4__

Fruit for Sale	
bananas	△△△△△△
apples	△△△△

Key: Each △ stands for 1 piece.

Balls in Box	
tennis balls	
baseballs	
soccer balls	

Key: Each ◯ stands for 2.

Balls in Box	
tennis balls	IIII
baseballs	IIII
soccer balls	II

1. Use the table to make a pictograph. Draw 1 ◯ for every 2 balls.

Use the information in the pictograph to solve.

2. How many more tennis balls are there than soccer balls?

_____

Spiral Review (Chapter 1 Lesson 3) **KEY** NS 2.1

Write the fact family for each set of numbers

3. 7, 8, 15   4. 8, 2, 10

_____   _____

_____   _____

Read a Picture Graph

CA Standards
SDAP 1.2, AF 1.3

Solve the problems using the picture graph.

Bears' Baseball Scores	Seals' Baseball Scores
Game 1 ○ ○ ○	Game 1 ○
Game 2 ○ ○ ○	Game 2 ○ ○
Game 3 ○ ○	Game 3 ○ ○ ○
Game 4 ○ ○ ○ ○ ○	Game 4 ○ ○
Each ○ stands for 1 point.	Each ○ stands for 2 points.

1. How many points did the Bears score in Game 2?

_____

2. How many points did the Seals score in Game 2?

_____

3. Which team scored more points in the second game?

_____

4. How many more points did the Bears score in Game 1 than the Seals?

_____

5. Which game or games did the Bears win by 2 points?

_____

6. Add one more ○ to each of the Seals games in the picture graph. How does that change the results for each game?

_____

_____

_____

Read and Make a Bar Graph

CA Standard
SDAP 1.2, SDAP 1.4

A bar graph can show the same data as a Tally chart.

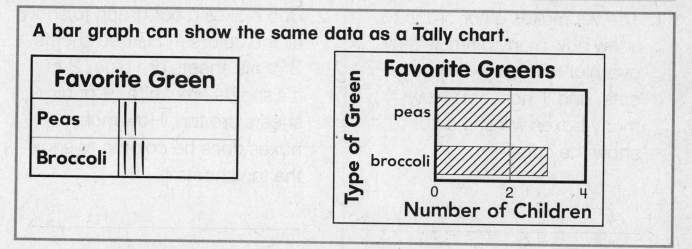

1. Use the tally chart to complete the bar graph.

Favorite Sports	
Soccer	IIII
Baseball	III
Running	IIII
Swimming	I

Favorite Sports

Sports: Soccer, Baseball, Running, Swimming
Number of Children: 0 1 2 3 4 5 6

Use the bar graph to answer the question.

2. How many children play baseball? _____

3. Which sport did the greatest number of children choose?

_____

4. Did more children choose baseball or running? _____

Spiral Review (Chapter 1, Lesson 4) **KEY NS 2.1**

Find the missing addend.

5. _____ $+ 3 = 7$ 6. $5 +$ _____ $= 10$ 7. _____ $+ 9 = 13$

Use with text pp. 29–30

Read and Make a Bar Graph

1. The vet makes a bar graph to show how many animals stay overnight. There are 6 dogs, 7 cats, and 1 hamster. How many boxes will she color to show the cats?

_____

2. Bob makes a bar graph to show all the colors of his bed sheets. 3 of his sheets are blue. 2 of his sheets are white. 4 of his sheets are tan. How many boxes does he color in to show the tan sheets?

_____

3. Matt makes a bar graph to show the life span of animals. A deer lives 8 years, a giraffe lives 10 years and a dog lives 12 years. How many more years does a dog live than a deer?

_____

4. Sally makes a bar graph to show her friends' favorite seasons. 2 like spring, 3 like fall, 4 like winter, and 8 like summer. How many more people like summer than winter?

_____

5. Sam makes a bar graph of his classmates' favorite sandwiches. 2 like cheese the best. 4 more students like bologna than cheese. 1 more person likes peanut butter and jelly than bologna. How many like peanut butter and jelly?

_____

6. Judy polls her friends for their favorite color. 5 like purple the best. 3 more people like blue than purple. 2 less people like yellow than blue the best. How many people like yellow?

_____

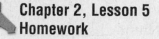
Range and Mode

CA Standard
SDAP 1.3, SDAP 1.4

Mrs. Hanson used a chart to mark the scores the students got on their math test.

Math Scores	
Score	Number of Students
100	3
98	2

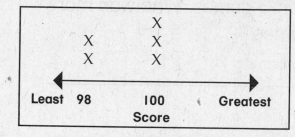

Write a number sentence to show the range of the data.

$$100 - 98 = 2$$

**Jack asked his classmates how long it takes them to eat their dinner.
Use the chart to answer the questions.**

Dinner Eating	
Minutes	Number of Students
10	5
20	2
30	6

1. How many students take the longest to eat their dinner?

_____

2. How many minutes do the fewest students take to eat?

_____ minutes

3. Write a number sentence to show the range of the data.

_____ − _____ = _____

(Chapter 1, Lesson 5) **AF 1.2**

4. Write a number sentence to solve. A squirrel collects 8 nuts, but drops 3 along the way. How many nuts does the squirrel have?

_____ ◯ _____ = _____

Range and Mode

CA Standard
SDAP 1.3, SDAP 1.4

1. Josh won 7 games, and Alice won 3 games. Who won more games?

_____

2. Jason ate 12 grapes, and Jeff ate 5 grapes. Who ate fewer grapes?

_____

3. Shirley has been riding horses for 7 years, Janice has been riding horses for 3 years, and Shane has been riding horses for 5 years. What is the difference between the greatest and the least number of years the girls rode horses?

_____ years

4. Sam lives 5 miles from school, Joe lives 2 miles from school, and Andy lives 1 mile from school. What is the range of the miles the boys live from school?

_____ miles

5. Craig reads a book with 10 pages in the morning, a book with 26 pages before dinner, and a book with 10 pages after dinner. Find the mode of the number of pages in the books that Craig read.

_____ pages

6. Robby runs for 5 minutes. He walks for 10 minutes. He runs for 7 minutes. He walks another 4 minutes. He runs again for 8 minutes and walks again for 3 minutes. What is the range of minutes Robby runs?

_____ minutes

Use a Graph

CA Standards
SDAP 1.4, AF 1.3

How many children choose strawberry and blueberries?

Favorite Berry

Number of children

8
6
4
2
0

strawberry   blueberry   raspberry
Types of Berries

Find the data in the bar graph and add.

$$\begin{array}{r} 6 \quad \text{strawberry} \\ + 4 \quad \text{blueberry} \\ \hline 10 \quad \text{in all} \end{array}$$

Mr. Morris took a survey of his class to find out their favorite juice.

Use the data in the graph to solve.

Favorite Fruit Juices

Number of Students

6
5
4
3
2
1
0

orange   grapefruit   grape   apple
juice   juice   juice   juice

Types of Juices

1. How many students like orange juice?

   _____

2. How many students like grape juice and apple juice?

   _____

3. How many students did Mr. Morris survey in all?

   _____

(Chapter 1, Lesson 5) **AF 1.2**

Write a number sentence to solve.

4. There are 7 monkeys jumping on a bed. 2 jump off. How many monkeys are jumping on the bed?

   _____ ◯ _____ = _____

Name _____ Date _____

Use a Graph

CA Standards
SDAP 1.4, AF 1.3

Use the data in the graph to solve.

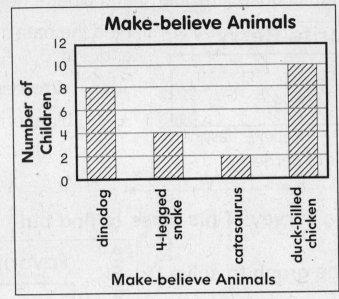

1. How many children like 4-legged snakes?

   _____ children

2. Do more children like the dinodog or the duck-billed chicken?

   _____

3. How many more children like dinodogs than 4-legged snakes?

   _____ children

4. How many more children like duck-billed chickens than 4-legged snakes?

   _____ children

5. 5 more children are added to the chart. 3 choose catasaurus, and the others choose dinodogs. How many children like catasaurus?

   _____ children

6. 4 children are taken off the chart. 2 children are removed from 4-legged snake, and the others from duck-billed chicken. How many like duck-billed chicken?

   _____ children

Hands On: Place Value to 200

CA Standards
KEY NS 1.1, NS 1.2

7 tens 3 ones

Tens	Ones
7	3

_73_
seventy-three

Write the tens and ones.
Then write the number.

I. 5 tens 7 ones

Tens	Ones

_____
fifty-seven

2. 4 tens 6 ones

Tens	Ones

_____
forty-six

3. 8 tens 1 ones

Tens	Ones

_____
eighty-one

4. 6 tens 0 ones

Tens	Ones

_____
sixty

Spiral Review (Chapter 2, Lesson 1) SDAP 1.1, **KEY** SDAP 1.0

Tara surveyed her class to find out how many staircases students have in their house.

Staircases	Tally Marks
0	IIII
I	II
2	III

5. What is the number of staircases most students have in their house? _____

6. How many students have 2 staircases? _____

Hands On: Place Value to 200

CA Standards
KEY NS 1.1, NS 1.2

Solve.

1. Write the number that has 5 tens and 3 ones.

   _____

2. Write the number that has 2 tens and 2 ones.

   _____

3. Tim counts his hockey cards. He puts them in 5 stacks of ten with 3 left over. How many hockey cards does Tim have?

   _____ hockey cards

4. Lucy buys beads to make necklaces. She puts beads in 3 groups of ten with 7 left over. How many beads does Lucy have?

   _____ beads

5. Ray and Anya count their video collection. Ray puts the cartoon videos in 2 groups of ten with 1 left over. Anya puts the video games in 1 group of ten with 5 left over. How many cartoon videos do they have?

   _____ cartoon videos

6. Casey has a collection of pennies. He puts them in 6 groups of ten with 5 left over. Then he gives 8 pennies to his brother. How many pennies does Casey have left?

   _____ pennies

Expanded Form

CA Standards
KEY NS 1.1, NS 1.2

To find the value of a digit, find the value of the place it is in.

Count how many.	Find the place of each digit.	Write the expanded form.	Write the number.
1.	_____ tens _____ ones	_____ + _____	_____
2.	_____ tens _____ ones	_____ + _____	_____
3.	_____ tens _____ ones	_____ + _____	_____

4. Luci has 23 flag stamps. What is the place value of the digits?

5. I have more ones than tens. The value of my tens digit is 80. What number am I?

_____ tens and _____ ones

_____

Spiral Review (Chapter 2, Lesson 2) **KEY** SDAP 1.0, AF 1.3

Jonathan surveys the 2nd and 3rd graders to find out which apples they like best.

2nd Grade		3rd Grade	
Green	10	Green	6
Red	4	Red	8

6. Which class likes green apples more?

_____

7. How many more students in the 2nd grade like green apples than students in the 3rd grade? _____

Expanded Form

1. What is the value of the tens digit in 54?

_____

2. What is the value of the ones digit in 27?

_____

3. A number has more ones than tens. The value of the tens digit is 60. What are the possible numbers?

_____

4. A number has more tens than ones. The value of the ones digit is 8. What are the possible numbers?

_____

5. A number has more ones than tens. The value of the tens digit is 50. The ones digit in the number is less than 7. What are the possible numbers?

_____

6. A number has more tens than ones, but the digit in the tens place is less than 4. The value of the ones digit is less than 3. What are the possible numbers?

_____

Hands On: Regroup Tens or Ones

CA Standards
KEY NS 1.1, MR 1.2

When you have 10 or more ones, you need to regroup.

Step ①	Step ②	Step ③
Show 31 as 2 tens 11 ones.	There are 11 ones. Regroup 10 ones as 1 ten.	This shows 31 as 3 tens and 1 one.

Show the tens and ones. Write the number.

1. 2 tens 17 ones   Regroup _____ tens _____ ones

2. 6 tens 16 ones   Regroup _____ tens _____ ones

Spiral Review   (Chapter 2, Lesson 3) **SDAP 1.2, AF 1.3**

Valentines Carol Made	
Grade 1	♡
Grade 2	♡ ♡

Key: Each ♡ counts as 3 valentines

3. How many valentines does Carol make in Grade 2? _____

4. How many valentines does Carol make in

   Grades 1 and 2? _____

Name _____ Date _____

Hands On: Regroup Tens or Ones

Make groups of 10 to solve.

1. James has 6 groups of 10 hats. How many hats does James have?

    _____ hats

2. Jackie has 3 groups of 10 stickers. How many stickers does Jackie have?

    _____ stickers

3. Sarah has 4 groups of 10 marbles and 15 marbles left over. How many marbles does Sarah have?

    _____ marbles

4. Jason has 6 stacks of 10 quarters and 18 quarters left over. How many quarters does James have?

    _____ quarters

5. Julia gives 5 of her friends 10 grapes each. She keeps 23 grapes for herself. How many grapes did Julia have to start?

    _____ grapes

6. The corner store has 4 packs with 10 pens each. They also have 31 extra pens. How many pens does the store have?

    _____ pens

Different Ways to Show Numbers

CA Standards
NS 1.2, NS 1.0

You can show a number in different ways.

22   20 + 2   2 tens
2 ones

Circle two ways to show the number.

1. 54		50 + 4	
2. 17	10 + 7	1 ten 7 ones	7 tens 1 one
3. 39		3 tens 9 ones	30 + 9

Spiral Review (Chapter 2, Lesson 4) **SDAP 1.2, SDAP 1.4**

Use the data in the bar graph to answer the questions.

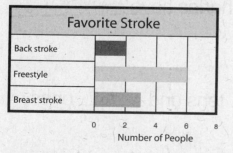

Favorite Stroke

Back stroke
Freestyle
Breast stroke

0 2 4 6 8
Number of People

4. Which stroke is the favorite?

_____

5. How many people like it the best? _____ people

Different Ways to Show Numbers

CA Standards
NS 1.2, NS 1.0

Show the answer 2 ways.

1. What is another way to show 36?

   _____ + _____

   _____ tens and _____ ones

2. What is another way to show 42?

   _____ + _____

   _____ tens and _____ ones

3. Hank has some markers. He puts the markers in 4 groups of 10 with 4 left over. How many markers does Hank have?

   _____

   _____ tens and _____ ones

4. Gwen has some little glow sticks. She puts the sticks in 1 group of 10 with 6 left over. How many little glow sticks does Gwen have?

   _____

   _____ ten and _____ ones

5. Marcy buys 3 boxes of blue beads and 2 boxes of red beads. There are 10 beads in each box. How many blue beads does Marcy have?

   _____

   _____ tens and _____ ones

6. Charles has some whistles. He puts the whistles in 5 groups of 10 with 3 left over. Then he buys another box of 10 whistles. How many whistles does Charles have?

   _____

   _____ tens and _____ ones

Find a Pattern

Making a table can help you find a pattern.

Look for a pattern. Then solve.
Explain your answers to a family member.

1. There are 3 books in a box.
   How many books are in 5 boxes?

Number of Boxes	1	2	3	4	5
Number of Books	3	6	9		

_____ books

2. Each jar has 4 pickles.
   How many pickles are in 4 jars?

Jars	1	2	3	4
Pickles	4	8		

_____ pickles

Spiral Review (Chapter 2, Lesson 5) **SDAP 1.3, SDAP 1.4**

Jack counted the number of wins the students had playing the ring toss.

Wins	
Number of Wins	Number of Students
0	5
1	2
2	6

3. What is the range of the number of wins?

   _____ − _____ = _____

4. What is the mode? _____

Name _____ Date _____

Find a Pattern

CA Standards
KEY SDAP 2.0, SDAP 2.2

Find a pattern to solve.

1. Jenna makes 2 snowmen. She puts 2 buttons on each for eyes. How many buttons does Jenna use?

   _____ buttons

2. Jenna then adds 1 carrot to each snowman for a nose. How many carrots does she use?

   _____ carrots

3. Sue has 6 dogs. Each dog has 4 legs. How many legs do the dogs have altogether?

   _____ legs

4. Bob has 3 cages of snakes in his room. Each cage has 3 snakes. How many snakes does Bob have?

   _____ snakes

5. Sam makes sock puppets. He uses 2 buttons for eyes and 1 button for a nose. How many buttons does he need for 6 puppets?

   _____ buttons

6. Max gives 5 people 5 cards each. Then he gives each person 1 more card. How many cards does Max hand out?

   _____ cards

Hands On:
Compare Numbers to 200

You can use place value to compare two numbers.

Compare 137 and 139.

First compare hundreds. 100 = 100

If the hundreds are equal, compare the tens. 30 = 30

If the tens are equal compare the ones. 7 is less than 9

137 is less than 139.

Compare the numbers.
Write the place value of each digit.
Circle to complete the sentence.

1. 165   162   2. 137   173

____, ____, ____ ____, ____, ____   ____, ____, ____ ____, ____, ____

greater than   greater than

165 is   162.   137 is   173.

less than   less than

Spiral Review (Chapter 3, Lesson 1) **KEY NS 1.1, NS 1.2**

Write the numbers.

3. 4 tens 7 ones   4. 7 tens 9 ones   5. 1 ten 3 ones

_____   _____   _____

Hands On:
Compare Numbers to 200

CA Standards
KEY NS 1.3, KEY NS 1.1

Compare the numbers to solve.

1. Jackie has 3 apples. Mary has 7 apples. Who has more apples?

   _____

2. Ted's house has 10 windows. Edward's house has 7 windows. Whose house has fewer windows?

   _____

3. Ivan has 147 books in his house. Carol has 152 books in her house. Who has more books?

   _____

4. Carter lives 179 miles from Florida and Nate lives 170 miles from Florida. Who lives closer to Florida?

   _____

5. Charlene has 147 red balloons and 119 blue balloons. Kate has 143 red balloons and 198 blue balloons. Who has more red balloons?

   _____

6. John collects 197 marbles. John also collects 162 stickers. Eric collects 165 stickers and 193 marbles. Who has more stickers?

   _____

Compare Numbers to 200

Use these symbols to compare numbers:

> greater than	< less than	= equal to

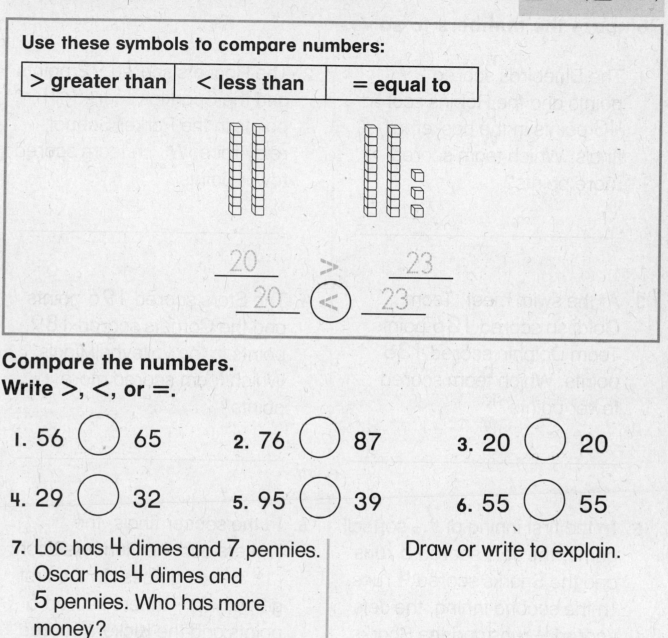

20 > 23
20 < 23

Compare the numbers.
Write >, <, or =.

1. 56 ◯ 65

2. 76 ◯ 87

3. 20 ◯ 20

4. 29 ◯ 32

5. 95 ◯ 39

6. 55 ◯ 55

7. Loc has 4 dimes and 7 pennies. Oscar has 4 dimes and 5 pennies. Who has more money?

Draw or write to explain.

_____

Spiral Review (Chapter 3, Lesson 2) **NS 1.2, KEY NS 1.1**

Circle the value of the underlined number.

8. 8<u>2</u>

9. 7<u>4</u>

10. <u>5</u>6

80   8

40   4

50   5

Compare Numbers to 200

Compare the numbers to solve.

1. The Bluebirds scored 29 points and the Robins scored 43 points in the basketball finals. Which team scored more points?

_____

2. The Rockets scored 92 points and the Sparkles scored 74 points in the Parker School relay race. Which team scored fewer points?

_____

3. At the swim meet, Team Goldfish scored 136 points. Team Dolphin scored 138 points. Which team scored fewer points?

_____

4. The Stars scored 196 points and the Comets scored 189 points in the volleyball finals. Which team scored more points?

_____

5. In the first inning of the softball game, the Jets scored 5 runs and the Sharks scored 4 runs. In the second inning, the Jets scored 4 runs and the Sharks scored 6 runs. Which team scored the most runs?

_____

6. In the soccer finals, the Kickers and the Runners each played two games. In the first game, the Runners scored 6 points and the Kickers scored 8 points. In the second game, the Kickers scored 4 points and the Runners scored 9 points. Which team scored the fewest points?

_____

Order Numbers to 200

CA Standards
KEY NS 1.3, KEY NS 1.1

Order 52, 50, and 48 from least to greatest.

52 |||||○○   50 ||||| 48 |||||○○○○
                                                ○○○○

Compare the tens, and then compare the ones.

The numbers from least to greatest are 48, 50, 52.

Write the numbers in order from least to greatest.

1. 18, 6, 12

_____, _____, _____

2. 55, 48, 42

_____, _____, _____

3. 76, 72, 78

_____, _____, _____

4. 85, 81, 77

_____, _____, _____

Write the numbers in order from greatest to least.

1. 46, 52, 16

_____, _____, _____

2. 68, 62, 67

_____, _____, _____

3. 39, 47, 35

_____, _____, _____

4. 93, 82, 89

_____, _____, _____

Spiral Review (Chapter 3, Lesson 3) **KEY NS 1.1, MR 1.2**

Regroup. Write the number.

10. 6 tens and 15 ones.

_____ tens and _____ ones

☐

11. 3 tens and 12 ones

_____ tens and _____ ones

☐

Name _____ Date _____

Order Numbers to 200

Solve.

1. Jay has 35 marbles and Jason has 37 marbles. Who has more marbles?

   _____

2. Sharron picks 53 apples and Susan picks 54 apples. Who picks fewer apples?

   _____

3. Cory lives 5 miles from school, Steven lives 7 miles from school, and Josh lives 3 miles from school. Who lives the closest to school?

   _____

4. Stuart reads for 67 minutes. Casey reads for 92 minutes. Caroline reads for 84 minutes. Who reads the longest?

   _____

5. Beth eats 3 oranges and 19 grapes. Mary eats 37 grapes and 1 orange. Ginger eats 7 oranges and 12 grapes. What is the middle amount of grapes eaten?

   _____ grapes

6. Karen has 6 pairs of shoes and 27 pairs of socks. Joan has 3 pairs of shoes and 45 pairs of socks. Ann has 8 pairs of shoes and 19 pairs of socks. Who has the middle amount of socks?

   _____

Use with text pp. 69–70

Round the Nearest Ten

CA Standard
NS 6.0

You can use a number line to round a number to the nearest ten.
Round 21 to the nearest ten.

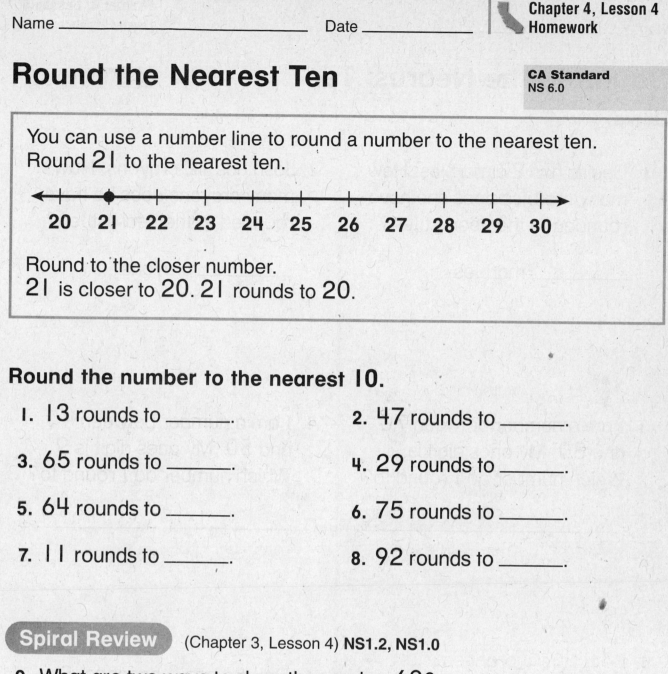

20 21 22 23 24 25 26 27 28 29 30

Round to the closer number.
21 is closer to 20. 21 rounds to 20.

Round the number to the nearest 10.

1. 13 rounds to _____.

2. 47 rounds to _____.

3. 65 rounds to _____.

4. 29 rounds to _____.

5. 64 rounds to _____.

6. 75 rounds to _____.

7. 11 rounds to _____.

8. 92 rounds to _____.

Spiral Review (Chapter 3, Lesson 4) **NS1.2, NS1.0**

9. What are two ways to show the number 69?

_____

_____

Name _____ Date _____

Round to the Nearest Ten

CA Standard
NS 6.0

Solve.

1. Cecilia has 27 marbles. How many marbles does she have rounded to the nearest ten?

_____ marbles

2. Josh has 12 crayons. How many crayons does he have rounded to the nearest ten?

_____ crayons

3. I am a number between 70 and 80. My ones digit is 2. Which number do I round to?

_____

4. I am a number between 40 and 50. My ones digit is 9. Which number do I round to?

_____

5. Adam has 8 stickers. His mother buys him 7 more. How many stickers does Adam have rounded to the nearest ten?

_____

6. Deirdre has 5 peaches. She picks 8 more peaches from the tree. How many peaches does Deirdre have rounded to the nearest ten?

_____

Reasonable Answers

> The most reasonable answer is the one that makes sense.
>
> Hassan and Brianna jump rope. Hassan jumps 25 times. Brianna jumps more than Hassan. About how many times could she have jumped?
>
> 15 times   22 times   (40 times)

Circle the most reasonable answer.
Explain your answers to a family member.

1. Glen visited his cousins 10 times last year. This year he visits his cousins more. About how many times does he visit his cousins?

   6 times   10 times   14 times

2. Oleg reads about 2 books every week. Ahman reads a few more books than that. About how many books does Ahman read every week?

   5 books   15 books   50 books

Spiral Review   (Chapter 3, Lesson 5) **KEY** SDAP 2.0, SDAP 2.2

Find a pattern to solve the problem.

3. James makes 4 smoothies. Each smoothie requires 2 cups of juice. How many cups of juice does James use in all?

   _____ cups of juice

4. Micaela has 3 bunches of bananas. Each bunch has 4 bananas. How many bananas does she have in all?

   _____ bananas

Reasonable Answers

Circle the most reasonable answer.

1. Jack has 17 marbles. Carey has a few more marbles than Jack has. How many marbles does Carey have?

   20   10   15

2. Victor lives 6 miles from school. Jane lives a few miles closer to school than Victor. How many miles from school does Jane live?

   10   8   3

3. Howard has 18 markers in his box. James has a few more markers in his box than Howard has. How many markers does James have?

   50   22   15

4. Will has 6 pillows on his bed. Carl has a few more pillows on his bed than Will. How many pillows does Carl have?

   4   35   8

5. Henry has 27 raisins in his lunch box. Lucy has 35 raisins in her lunch box. Nancy has a few more raisins in her lunch box than Henry and a few less than Lucy. How many raisins does Nancy have?

   30   45   20

6. Shaina drives 17 miles to go to the store. Ellen drives 29 miles to go to the store. Kim drives a few miles less than Shaina to go to the store. How many miles does Kim drive to the store?

   10   25   30

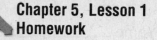
Hands On: Count by 2s

CA Standards
SDAP 2.1, KEY SDAP 2.0

You can use a hundred chart to skip count by 2s.

Use the hundred chart.

1. Skip count by 2s. Color in the numbers.

Use the hundred chart to complete the pattern.

2. 56, 58, ___, ___, 64, ___, ___, 70

3. 69, 71, ___, ___, 77, 79, ___, ___,

   ___

4. 34, 36, ___, ___, ___, 44, 46, ___

1	2	3	4	5	6	7	8	9	10
11	12	13	14	15	16	17	18	19	20
21	22	23	24	25	26	27	28	29	30
31	32	33	34	35	36	37	38	39	40
41	42	43	44	45	46	47	48	49	50
51	52	53	54	55	56	57	58	59	60
61	62	63	64	65	66	67	68	69	70
71	72	73	74	75	76	77	78	79	80
81	82	83	84	85	86	87	88	89	90
91	92	93	94	95	96	97	98	99	100

Spiral Review (Chapter 4, Lesson 1) **KEY** NS 1.3, **KEY** NS 1.1

Write the value of the digits.
Circle to complete the sentence.

5. 47   43

   ___, ___   ___, ___

   47   is greater than 43.

   is less than

6. 58   63

   ___, ___   ___, ___

   58   is greater than 63.

   is less than

Hands On: Count by 2s

CA Standards
SDAP 2.1, KEY SDAP 2.0

Count by 2s to solve.

1. Beth counts by 2. She starts with 2, then 4. What 3 numbers come next?

   _____

2. Tim counts by 2 on a hundred chart. He starts with 1, then 3. Which 3 numbers does he count next?

   _____

3. Kelly is counting by 2 on a hundred chart. She is to circle the numbers counting by 2, starting with 12. What are the next 3 numbers Kelly circles?

   _____

4. Ken is told to put an X on the numbers he counts on a hundred chart. He is counting by 2. He starts with 27. What are the next 3 numbers Ken puts X's on?

   _____

5. Jim is counting by 2s on a hundred chart. He makes a mark on 28. Which 2 numbers did Jim make a mark on before 28?

   _____

6. Caitlin is counting by 2s on a hundred chart. She is told to skip every number that has an 8 in it. She starts with the number 6. What are the next 3 numbers Caitlin counts?

   _____

Count by 5s

CA Standard
SDAP 2.1

Skip counting on a hundred chart shows different number patterns.

Use the hundred chart.

1. Count by 5s.
   Color the numbers red.

1	2	3	4	5	6	7	8	9	10
11	12	13	14	15	16	17	18	19	20
21	22	23	24	25	26	27	28	29	30
31	32	33	34	35	36	37	38	39	40
41	42	43	44	45	46	47	48	49	50
51	52	53	54	55	56	57	58	59	60
61	62	63	64	65	66	67	68	69	70
71	72	73	74	75	76	77	78	79	80
81	82	83	84	85	86	87	88	89	90
91	92	93	94	95	96	97	98	99	100

Follow the pattern.
Write the missing numbers.

2. 30, 40, 50, 60, ___, 80, ___, 100

3. 27, 32, 37, 42, ___, 52, ___, 62

4. ▯▯▯■▯▯▯■▯▯▯■

Which boxes follow the pattern? Circle the answer.

■▯▯■ ▯▯▯■ ▯■▯■

Spiral Review (Chapter 4, Lesson 2) **KEY** NS 1.3, **KEY** NS 1.1

Compare the numbers using >, <, or =.

5. 65 ◯ 64   6. 28 ◯ 28   7. 37 ◯ 47

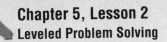
Count by 5s

CA Standard
SDAP 2.1

Read. Then solve.
Use a hundred chart if you wish.

1. Lauren writes a number pattern. The first four numbers are 2, 4, 6, 8. What two numbers does she write next? (Hint: count by 2s.)

_____

2. Kevin is trying to find the next two numbers of a number pattern. The pattern is 5, 10, 15, 20, 25. What are the next two numbers? (Hint: count by 5s.)

_____

3. Ana and Sam play a pattern game. Ana writes this number pattern: 76, 78, 80, 82. Sam must write the next two numbers in the pattern. What numbers should he write?

_____

4. Jasmine makes a set of number cards. The cards follow a pattern. The first four cards are numbered 45, 50, 55, 60. What are the next three number cards she will make?

_____

5. Jay writes a different number on a T-shirt for each person on the math team. Jay's number is 4. Each of the other numbers has 4 or 9 in the ones place. What number did Jay count by to choose the numbers?

_____

6. Scott has 2 pairs of gloves. Each glove has 5 fingers. How many fingers are there in all?

_____ fingers

Count by 10s

CA Standard
SDAP 2.1

You can use a hundred chart to skip count by 10.
Start on 10. Color it.
Skip count by 10s and color the numbers.

1	2	3	4	5	6	7	8	9	10
11	12	13	14	15	16	17	18	19	20
21	22	23	24	25	26	27	28	29	30
31	32	33	34	35	36	37	38	39	40
41	42	43	44	45	46	47	48	49	50
51	52	53	54	55	56	57	58	59	60
61	62	63	64	65	66	67	68	69	70
71	72	73	74	75	76	77	78	79	80
81	82	83	84	85	86	87	88	89	90
91	92	93	94	95	96	97	98	99	100

Use the hundred chart to complete the patterns.

1. 20, 30, ___, ___, ___

2. 45, 55, ___, ___, ___

3. 27, 37, ___, ___, ___

4. What do you notice about the ones digits in problem 2?

_____

Spiral Review (Chapter 4, Lesson 3) **NS 1.3, KEY NS 1.1**

Write the numbers from least to greatest.

5. 57 63 49 _____   6. 128 146 139 _____

Count by 10s

CA Standard
SDAP 2.1

Skip count by 10s to solve each problem.

1. Kendra wants to practice counting by 10s. She starts counting 10, 20, and then she gets stuck. Help Kendra figure out what the next 3 numbers should be.

_____

2. Scott decided to challenge himself and count by 10s starting with a random number. He starts with 47, then counts 57, and then gets stuck. Help Scott to find the next 3 numbers.

_____

3. Charlene makes 6 bunches of 10 flowers. She counts by 10s to find the number of flowers. How many flowers does Charlene use?

_____ flowers

4. Greg has 4 boxes of crayons. Each box has 10 crayons. Greg counts by 10s to find the number of crayons. How many crayons does Greg have?

_____ crayons

5. Steve has 8 bags with 10 yellow marbles each. He also has 2 bags with 10 purple marbles each. How many marbles does Steve have?

_____ marbles

6. Shelly has 5 bowls with ten pieces of fruit in each. She also has 8 bunches of celery. How many pieces of fruit does Shelly have?

_____ pieces of fruit

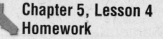
Even and Odd Numbers

CA Standards
SDAP 2.1, SDAP 2.2

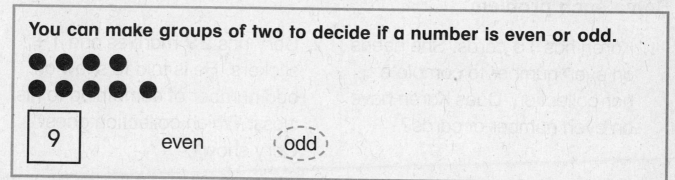

You can make groups of two to decide if a number is even or odd.

9   even   (odd)

Draw dots. Make groups of two to show the number.
Circle even or odd.

Dots

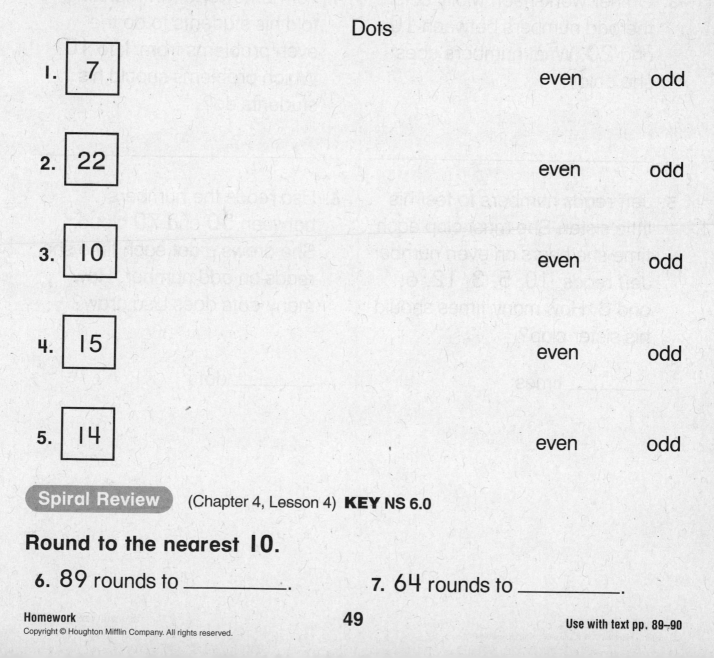

1. 7   even   odd

2. 22   even   odd

3. 10   even   odd

4. 15   even   odd

5. 14   even   odd

Spiral Review (Chapter 4, Lesson 4) **KEY** NS 6.0

Round to the nearest 10.

6. 89 rounds to _____.

7. 64 rounds to _____.

Even and Odd Numbers

CA Standards
SDAP 2.1, SDAP 2.2

Solve each problem.

1. Karen has 15 cards. She needs an even number to complete her collection. Does Karen have an even number of cards?

   _____

2. Cory has 29 marbles and 14 stickers. He is told to show an odd number of something to his class. Which collection does Cory show?

   _____

3. On her worksheet, Molly colors the odd numbers between 10 and 20. What numbers does she color?

   _____

4. For homework, Mr. Manning told his students to do the even problems from 1 to 10. Which problems should his students do?

   _____

5. Jeff reads numbers to test his little sister. She must clap each time she hears an even number. Jeff reads: 10, 5, 3, 12, 6, and 8. How many times should his sister clap?

   _____ times

6. Lisa reads the numbers between 50 and 70 aloud. She draws a dot each time she reads an odd number. How many dots does Lisa draw?

   _____ dots

Create and Solve

CA Standards
SDAP 2.2, KEY SDAP 2.0

You can write problems and use strategies from the math you know to solve them.

Lisa and Sam play a guessing game with the hundred chart.
Lisa writes these riddles.
Try to solve Lisa's riddles.

1	2	3	4	5	6	7	8	9	10
11	12	13	14	15	16	17	18	19	20
21	22	23	24	25	26	27	28	29	30
31	32	33	34	35	36	37	38	39	40
41	42	43	44	45	46	47	48	49	50
51	52	53	54	55	56	57	58	59	60
61	62	63	64	65	66	67	68	69	70
71	72	73	74	75	76	77	78	79	80
81	82	83	84	85	86	87	88	89	90
91	92	93	94	95	96	97	98	99	100

1. When I start at 10 and count by 10s, I land on the secret number. The secret number is not 10. The secret number is less than 30. What is the secret number?

   _____

2. When I start at 6 and count by 2s, I land on the secret number. The secret number is not 2. The secret number is less than 20. The secret number has 2 in the ones place. What is the secret number?

   _____

3. When I start at 3 and count by 5s, I land on the secret number. The secret number is not 3. The secret number is less than 15. The secret number is even. What is the secret number?

   _____

Spiral Review   (Chapter 4, Lesson 5) **NS 1.0, AF 1.0**

4. Ned picks 5 flowers. Jill picks a few more flowers than Ned. Circle how many flowers Jill picks.

   3   7   20

5. Rosa has 24 crayons. Juan has a few less crayons than Rosa. Circle how many crayons Juan has.

   25   12   21

Use with text pp. 91–92

Create and Solve

CA Standards
SDAP 2.2, KEY SDAP 2.0

Solve the riddles. Use the hundred chart to help you.

1. I start at 2 and count by 2s. The next number after 8 is the secret number. What is the secret number?

_____

2. I start at 10 and count by 10s. The next number I count is the secret number. What is the secret number?

_____

3. When I start at 6 and count by 2's, I land on the secret number. The secret number is less than 20. The secret number has 4 in the ones place. What is the secret number?

_____

4. When I start at 25 and count by 5s, I land on the secret number. The secret number is not 25. The secret number is less than 40. The secret number is even. What is the secret number?

_____

5. When I start at 3 and count by 5s, I land on the secret number. The secret number is not 3. The secret number is less than 20. The secret number is the number after the number that has an 8 in the ones place. What is the secret number?

_____

6. When I start at 6 and count by 5s, I land on the secret number. The secret number is not 6. The secret number is less than 20. The secret number comes after the number with an odd digit in the ones place. What is the secret number?

_____

Hands On: Identify Coins

Write the name and value of each coin.

half-dollar	quarter	dime	nickel	penny
50 ¢	25 ¢	10 ¢	5 ¢	1 ¢

Write the coin values. Draw the coins in order from greatest value to least value.

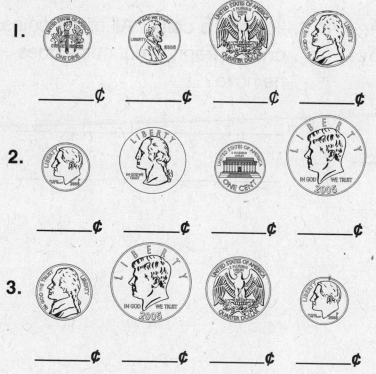

1. _____ ¢ _____ ¢ _____ ¢ _____ ¢

2. _____ ¢ _____ ¢ _____ ¢ _____ ¢

3. _____ ¢ _____ ¢ _____ ¢ _____ ¢

Use with text pp. 105–106

Hands On: Identify Coins

CA Standard
KEY NS 5.2, MR 1.2

Solve the problems.

1. Seth has one dime. How much money does he have?

   _____ ¢

2. Todd has a coin worth 25¢. What type of coin does he have?

   _____

3. Alison has a dime, a nickel, and 2 pennies. What is the value of the dime?

   _____ ¢

4. Matt has 2 dimes, 3 nickels, and 4 pennies. What is the value of the pennies?

   _____ ¢

5. Roberta has some coins. They have these values: 10¢, 25¢, 1¢. What coins does she have?

   _____

   _____

6. Jay has 5 coins. All of the coins are different. What coins does he have?

   _____

   _____

Hands On: Count Coins

CA Standard
KEY NS 5.1, **KEY** NS 5.2

When you count on to find the value of the coins, first put the coins in order. Start with the coin with the greatest value.

_50_ ¢   _75_ ¢   _80_ ¢   _81_ ¢   _82_ ¢

Put the coins in order from greatest to least value. Then find the total value of the coins.

1. _____ ¢

2. _____ ¢

3. _____ ¢

4. _____ ¢

Spiral Review   (Chapter 5, Lesson 2) **SDAP 2.1**

Count by 5s. Write the missing numbers.

5. 20, 25, _____, _____, 40, 45, _____, _____

6. 11, 16, 21, _____, _____, _____, 41, _____

Hands On: Count Coins

Find the values. Draw or use coins to help you.

1. Kate has 2 dimes. How much money does she have?

   _____ ¢

2. Kevin has 3 pennies. How much money does he have?

   _____ ¢

3. Corin has 2 quarters and 3 dimes. What is the value of her coins?

   _____ ¢

4. Caleb has 3 dimes, 2 nickels, and 1 penny. What is the value of his coins?

   _____ ¢

5. Sarah has 65¢. She has 4 coins. Which coins does she have?

   _____

   _____

6. Steve has 47¢. He has 6 coins. Which coins does he have?

   _____

   _____

Hands On: Equal Amounts

CA Standard
KEY NS 5.1, NS 5.0

Different sets of coins can make equal amounts.
You can show two ways to make **75¢**.

75¢   75¢

**Show two ways to make the amount shown.
Draw the coins.**

	1. 69¢	2. 69¢
69¢		
	3. 87¢	4. 87¢
87¢		

Spiral Review (Chapter 5, Lesson 3) **SDAP 2.1**

Count by 10s. Write the missing numbers.

5. 37, 47, _____, _____, _____, _____

6. 22, _____, 42, _____, _____, _____, 82

Hands On: Equal Amounts

CA Standards
KEY NS 5.1, NS 5.0

Solve each problem. Draw coins to help you.

1. Kyle has 50¢. He only has quarters. How many quarters does Kyle have?

   _____ quarters

2. Sue has 20¢. She only has nickels. How many nickels does Sue have?

   _____ nickels

3. Stuart has 2 piles of coins. Each pile has a value of 55¢. One pile has 2 quarters and 1 nickel. What coins could the other pile have?

   _____

   _____

4. Ruth has 2 piles of coins. Each pile has a value of 23¢. One pile has 2 dimes and 3 pennies. What coins could the other pile have?

   _____

   _____

5. Ken has 2 piles of coins. Each pile has a value of 56¢. One pile has 4 coins and the other pile has 5 coins. Which coins do the piles have?

   First pile: _____

   _____

   Second pile: _____

   _____

6. Kendra has 2 piles of coins. Each pile has a value of 88¢. One pile has 7 coins, and the other pile has 6 coins. Which coins do the piles have?

   First pile: _____

   _____

   Second pile: _____

   _____

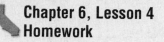
Compare Money Amounts

CA Standards
KEY NS 5.1, **KEY** NS 5.2

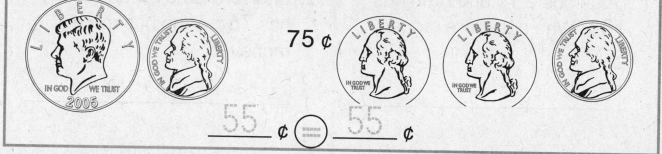

You can compare the values of two sets of coins.
Write the value of each set of coins. Compare. Write >, <, or =.

75 ¢

_55_ ¢ ( ) _55_ ¢

Write the value of each set of coins. Compare the sets.

1.

_____ ¢ ◯ _____ ¢

2.

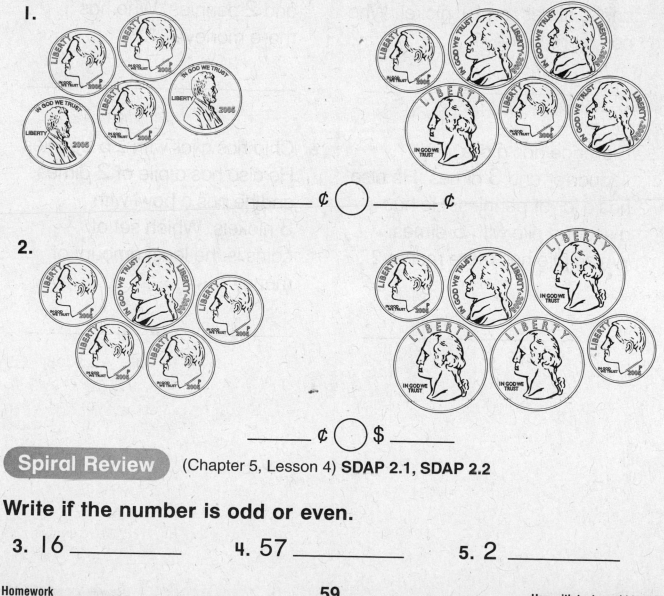

_____ ¢ ◯ $ _____

Spiral Review (Chapter 5, Lesson 4) **SDAP 2.1, SDAP 2.2**

Write if the number is odd or even.

3. 16 _____   4. 57 _____   5. 2 _____

Compare Money Amounts

CA Standards
KEY NS 5.1, **KEY** NS 5.2

Solve each problem. Draw coins to help you.

1. Hugh has 24¢ and Beth has 15¢. Who has more money?

   _____

2. Sharron has 67¢ and Hilary has 76¢. Who has more money?

   _____

3. Hector has 2 quarters and 2 dimes. Jean has 3 quarters and 2 dimes, and 1 nickel. Who has more money?

   _____

4. Jason has 3 dimes and 2 pennies. Claire has 5 nickels and 2 pennies. Who has more money?

   _____

5. Clarence has a pile with 1 quarter and 3 dimes. He also has a jar of pennies. He has a second pile with 6 dimes. Which pile has more money?

   _____

6. Chip has a jar with 26 pennies. He also has a pile of 2 dimes and he has a bowl with 3 nickels. Which set of coins is the least amount of money?

   _____

Make a List

Making a list can sometimes help you solve a problem.

Michail wants a toy car that costs 50¢. He has quarters and nickels. He makes a list to find the ways he can make 50¢

He can make 50¢ three ways.

Use coins to solve.
Complete the list.

1. Maria wants a toy. It costs 15¢. She has dimes, nickels, and pennies. How many ways can Maria make 15¢?

   Maria can make 15¢ _____ ways.

Spiral Review (Chapter 5, Lesson 5) **SDAP 2.2, KEY SDAP 2.0**

Solve each riddle.

2. When I start at 5 and count by 5s, I land on this number.
   The number is not 5.
   The number is less than 20.
   The number is odd.
   What is the number? _____

3. When I start at 2 and count by 2s, I land on this number.
   The number is not 16.
   The number is more than 15.
   The number is less than 20.
   What is the number? _____

61

Make a List

Make a list to help you solve the problems.

1. Kate has only nickels and dimes. She wants to buy a bunch of bananas for 35¢. Show one way Kate can make 35¢.

Dimes	Nickels

2. Elise has only pennies. She wants to buy a book for 10¢. How many pennies does she need to make 10¢?

_____ pennies

3. Jeffrey wants to buy a poster that costs 15¢. He only has nickels and pennies. Show 2 or more ways he can make 15¢.

Nickels	Pennies

4. Louis wants to buy an apple. The apple costs 37¢. He only has quarters, dimes and pennies. Show 2 or more ways he can make 37¢.

Quarters	Dimes	Pennies

5. Chuck wants to buy some markers for 30¢. He has nickels and quarters and pennies. He does not want to use his pennies. Show the ways he can make 30¢.

Quarters	Nickels

6. Dora wants to buy a bottle of soap for 29¢. She has quarters, dimes, nickels, and pennies. She does not want to use the dimes. How many ways can Dora make 29¢?

_____ ways

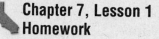
Hands On: Use Coins to Show an Amount

Circle the coins that make the exact amount.

1. 75¢

2. 48¢

3. 61¢

 Spiral Review (Chapter 6, Lesson 1) **KEY** NS 5.2, MR 1.2

Write the value of the coins.

4. 1 quarter

5. 2 dimes

6. 4 nickels

_____   _____   _____

Hands On: Use Coins to Show an Amount

CA Standards
KEY NS 5.1, NS 5.0

Solve.

1. Ben wants to buy an eraser for 12¢. He already has 1 dime. How much more money does he need in order to buy the eraser?

_____

2. Pablo wants to buy a notebook for 30¢. He only has 1 quarter. How much more money does he need in order to buy the notebook?

_____

3. Neena wants to buy a book for 92¢. She has 2 quarters, 2 dimes, and 2 nickels. How much more money does she need?

_____

4. Jen wants to buy a tape for 47¢. She has 1 quarter, 1 nickel, and 2 pennies. How much more money does Jen need?

_____

5. Cameron has 2 quarters, 4 dimes, and 3 pennies. She wants to buy a board game for 91¢. Which coins does she not need in order to buy the game?

_____

6. Sam wants to buy a lamp for 85¢. He has 2 quarters, 3 dimes, and 5 nickels. Which coins does he not need in order to buy the lamp?

_____

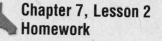
Use Money

CA Standards
KEY NS 5.1, NS 5.0

You can use the fewest coins to show an amount of money.

37¢

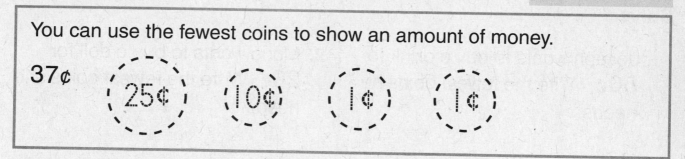

Draw the fewest coins that show the amount.

1. 66¢

_____

2. 95¢

_____

3. 47¢

Spiral Review   (Chapter 6, Lesson 2) **KEY** NS 5.1, **KEY** NS 5.2

Put the coins in order from greatest to least value.
Count on to find the value of the coins.

4.   5.

_____ ¢   _____ ¢

          Use with text pp. 125–126

Use Money

Solve.

1. Joseph wants to buy a drink for 50¢. Write the fewest coins he needs.

   _____

2. Maria wants to buy a doll for 20¢. Write the fewest coins she needs.

   _____

3. Helen wants to buy a plant for 83¢. Write the fewest coins she needs.

   _____

   _____

4. Adam wants to buy some blocks for 75¢. Write the fewest coins he needs.

   _____

5. Jessica wants to buy a basket for 97¢. What is the fewest number of coins she needs?

   _____ coins

6. Aaron wants to buy a hammer for 77¢. What is the fewest number of coins he needs?

   _____ coins

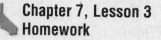
One Dollar

CA Standards
KEY NS 5.2, **KEY** NS 5.1

> 100¢ has the same value as one dollar. 100¢ is written as $1.00.
> You use a dollar sign ($) and a decimal point (.) to show the amount.

Write the value of the coins.
Circle the sets of coins that equal one dollar.

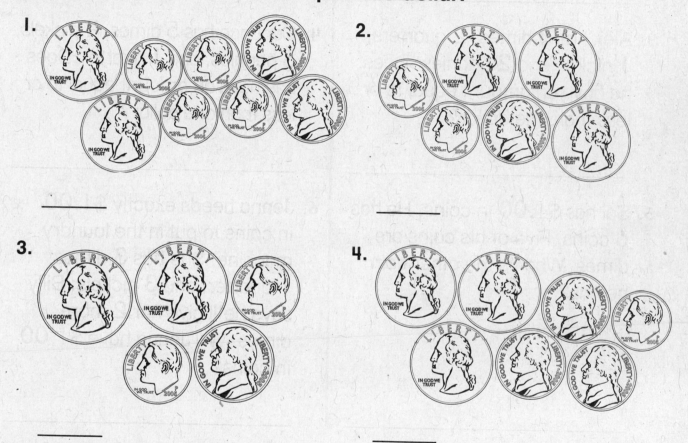

1. _____

2. _____

3. _____

4. _____

Spiral Review (Chapter 6, Lesson 3) **KEY** NS 5.1, NS 5.0

Draw the coins.

5. Show 73¢.

6. Show 73¢ another way.

One Dollar

CA Standards
KEY NS 5.2, **KEY** NS 5.1

Solve.

1. Maya has 97¢. Does she have more or less than $1.00?

_____

2. Louis has 125¢. Does he have more or less than $1.00?

_____

3. Alex has 3 dimes, 2 quarters, 1 nickel, and 2 pennies. Does he have an amount equal to or less than one dollar?

_____

4. Candace has 5 dimes, 4 nickels, 5 pennies, and 1 quarter. Does she have an amount equal to or less than one dollar?

_____

5. Sal has $1.00 in coins. He has 6 coins. Five of his coins are dimes. What is the other coin he has?

_____

6. Jenna needs exactly $1.00 in coins to put in the laundry machine. She has 3 dimes, 1 quarter, and 3 nickels. Billy says he'll give her 2 more dimes. Will Jenna have $1.00 in coins?

_____

Make Change

CA Standards
KEY NS 5.1, NS 5.0

When you pay more money than the price, you get change. You can count on from the price to find the change.

Amount Paid	Price	Draw Coins to Count On			Change
25 ¢	22	23 ¢	24 ¢	25 ¢	3 ¢

Write the amount paid.

Draw the coins and count on to find the change.

Amount Paid	Price	Draw Coins to Count On		Change
1. _____ ¢	44¢	_____ ¢	_____ ¢	_____ ¢
2. $_____	85¢	_____ ¢	_____ ¢ $_____	_____ ¢

Spiral Review   (Chapter 6, Lesson 4) **KEY** NS 5.1, **KEY** NS 5.2

Write the value of the set of coins. Compare the sets.

3.

_____ ◯ _____

Name _____ Date _____

Make Change

CA Standards
KEY NS 5.1, NS 5.0

Solve.

1. Adam buys some grapes for 25¢. He pays 30¢. How much change does he receive?

_____ ¢

2. Josh buys a coconut for 50¢. He pays 60¢. How much change does he receive?

_____ ¢

3. Regina buys a peach for 28¢. She pays with 1 quarter and 1 dime. How much change does she receive?

_____ ¢

4. Jamal buys an orange for 42¢. He pays with 1 half dollar. How much change does he receive?

_____ ¢

5. Ellen buys a mango for 53¢. She pays with 2 quarters and 1 dime. How many pennies and nickels does she get as change?

_____

_____

6. Shanika buys an apple for 37¢. She pays with one half dollar. How many pennies and nickels does she get as change?

_____

_____

Leveled Problem Solving
70
Use with text pp. 129–132

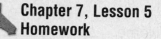

Act It Out

CA Standards
NS 5.0, MR 2.0

Sometimes you can act with models to solve a problem.
One way is to use coins to show amounts of money.

**Use coins to act out the problem.   Draw or write to explain.
Solve.**

1. Delia has 2 quarters and 2 dimes. She wants to buy a ball for 60¢. Does she have enough money?

   _____

2. Nick is saving to buy flowers for his mother. He has 2 quarters, 1 dime, and 3 nickels. This is the same price as the flowers. How much are the flowers?

   _____

Spiral Review   (Chapter 6, Lesson 5) **KEY NS 5.1, SDAP 1.1**

Use coins to solve. Make a list.

3. Chris has quarters and nickels. How many ways can he make 60¢?

Quarters	Nickels

   _____ ways

4. Hannah has dimes and nickels. How many ways can she make 40¢?

   _____ ways

Name _____ Date _____

Act It Out

Use coins to help you solve the problems.

1. Sally wants to buy a new book. She has 1 quarter and 2 dimes. This is the price of the book. How much does the book cost?

_____ ¢

2. Casey wants to buy a new keychain. He has 3 dimes and 1 nickel. This is the same price as the keychain. How much does the keychain cost?

_____ ¢

3. Gwen has 1 quarter, 2 dimes, and 3 pennies, How much more money does she need to buy a hand puppet for 58¢?

_____ ¢

4. Dan has 2 quarters and 3 dimes. He buys a pair of socks for 72¢. How much change does he receive?

_____ ¢

5. Esther buys some pens for 37¢ and stickers for 10¢. She pays $1.00. How much change does she get back?

_____ ¢

6. Al buys some glue for 53¢ and some paper for 22¢. He pays $1.00. How much change does he get back?

_____ ¢

Hands On: Add Tens

CA Standard
KEY NS 2.2, NS 2.3

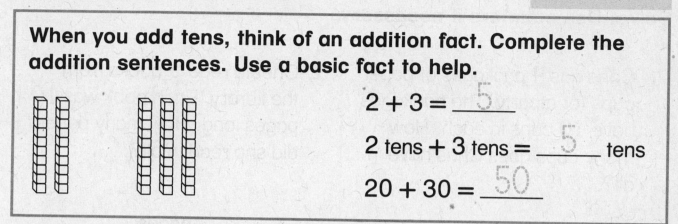

When you add tens, think of an addition fact. Complete the addition sentences. Use a basic fact to help.

$2 + 3 =$ ___5___

2 tens $+ 3$ tens $=$ ___5___ tens

$20 + 30 =$ ___50___

Complete the addition sentences. Use a basic fact to help.

1. 4 tens $+ 4$ tens $=$ _____ tens

_____ $+$ _____ $=$ _____

2. 1 ten $+ 3$ tens $=$ _____ tens

_____ $+$ _____ $=$ _____

3. 6 tens $+ 3$ tens $=$ _____ tens

_____ $+$ _____ $=$ _____

4. 3 tens $+ 5$ tens $=$ _____ tens

_____ $+$ _____ $=$ _____

5. Katie has 5 sheets of stickers. There are 10 stickers on each sheet. Her sister Rory gives her 2 sheets more. How many stickers does Katie have in all?

_____ stickers

Spiral Review   (Chapter 7, Lesson 1) **NS 5.0, KEY NS 5.1**

6. Mike has 20¢. Write two ways to make the exact amount.

_____

Name _____ Date _____

Hands On: Add Tens

CA Standards
KEY NS 2.2, NS 2.3

Solve. Use counters if necessary.

1. Chris has 4 packages of paper cups for a party. The packages have 10 cups in each. How many cups does Chris have in all?

_____ cups

2. Gheeta read 5 books from the library. Each book was 10 pages long. How many pages did she read in all?

_____ pages

3. A store has boxes with 10 pencils in each. Ms. Flores buys 3 boxes of colored pencils and 5 boxes of plain pencils. How many pencils does Ms. Flores have in all?

_____ pencils

4. Max has 4 packs of baseball trading cards with 10 cards in each pack. He has 3 packs of basketball trading cards with 10 cards in each pack. How many trading cards does Max have in all?

_____ trading cards

5. Rosa has 7 sheets of clown stickers. She has 2 sheets of acrobat stickers. Each sheet has 10 stickers. She has one sheet with 10 juggler stamps. How many stickers does Rosa have in all?

_____ stickers

6. Ralph goes to the store and buys 3 bags of hotdog rolls and 4 bags of hamburger rolls. Each bag contains 10 rolls. He also buys 10 pounds of hamburger meat. How many rolls does he buy in all?

_____ rolls

Add Tens and Ones

CA Standard
KEY NS 2.2

When you have 10 or more ones, you need to regroup.

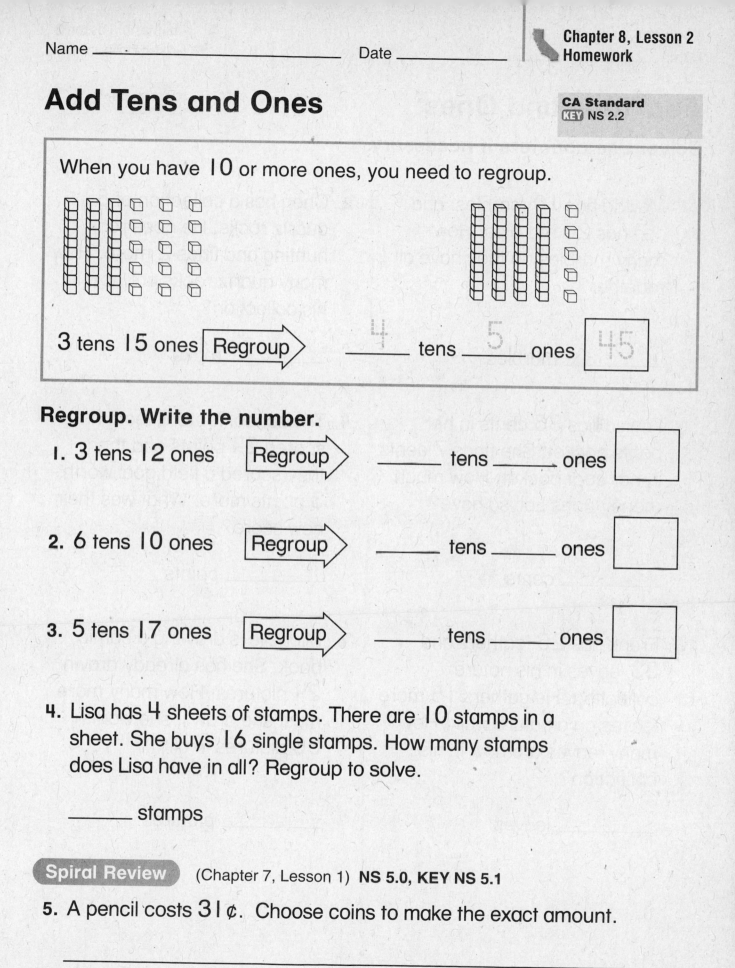

3 tens 15 ones [Regroup] ___4___ tens ___5___ ones [45]

Regroup. Write the number.

1. 3 tens 12 ones [Regroup] _____ tens _____ ones [ ]

2. 6 tens 10 ones [Regroup] _____ tens _____ ones [ ]

3. 5 tens 17 ones [Regroup] _____ tens _____ ones [ ]

4. Lisa has 4 sheets of stamps. There are 10 stamps in a sheet. She buys 16 single stamps. How many stamps does Lisa have in all? Regroup to solve.

_____ stamps

Spiral Review   (Chapter 7, Lesson 1) NS 5.0, KEY NS 5.1

5. A pencil costs 31¢. Choose coins to make the exact amount.

Use with text pp. 151–152

Add Tens and Ones

Solve. Use counters if necessary.

1. Martha has 10 marbles, and Joe has 20 marbles. How many marbles do they have all together?

   _____ marbles

2. Chen has a collection of 8 quartz rocks. He goes rock hunting and finds 2 more. How many quartz rocks are now in his collection?

   _____ rocks

3. Louisa has 35 cents in her pants pocket. She finds 7 cents in her coat pocket. How much money does Louisa have?

   _____ cents

4. The school football team had scored 24 points and then they scored a field goal worth 3 points more. What was their new score?

   _____ points

5. Frank has 25 feathers and 33 leaves in his nature collection. He gathers 15 more leaves on a nature walk. How many leaves are now in his collection?

   _____ leaves

6. Michelle is drawing a comic book. She has already drawn 24 pictures. How many more must she draw if she wants 30 pictures in all?

   _____ pictures

Name _____ Date _____

Hands On: Model Adding 2-Digit Numbers

CA Standard
KEY NS 2.2, MR 1.2

Solve. Use 10 attached ▭▭▭▭▭ to show tens.

Use single ▢ to show ones. If there are 10 or more ones, you need to regroup.

	Show both numbers.	Add the ones. How many tens and ones are there?	Do you need to regroup?	What is the sum?
1.	16 + 9	___1___ ten ___15___ ones	(Yes) No	25
2.	39 + 4	_____ tens _____ ones	Yes No	
3.	24 + 5	_____ tens _____ ones	Yes No	

4. Place 29 beans in rows of 10, 10, and 9. Then add 8 more beans. How many beans do you have in all? Regroup to solve.

_____ beans

Spiral Review (Chapter 7, Lesson 4) **NS 5.0**

5. A comb on sale costs 39¢. Ruth pays for it with 50¢. How much change does she get back?

_____

Use with text pp. 153–154

Hands On: Model Adding 2-Digit Numbers

CA Standard
KEY NS 2.2, MR 1.2

Solve.

1. Arthur has 20 pennies. He returns four bottles and gets 20 more pennies. How many pennies does Arthur have in all?

   _____ pennies

2. Mimi has a box with 40 crayons. She works with Elise, who has 20 crayons. How many crayons do they have together?

   _____ crayons

3. Jamal rode his bike for 25 minutes on Wednesday and for 23 minutes on Thursday. How many minutes did he ride all together?

   _____ minutes

4. Robin finds she has 18 barrettes in one box and 16 barrettes in another. How many barrettes does she have in all?

   _____ barrettes

5. LaDonna read 24 pages from a book that is 44 pages long. How many more pages does she have to read?

   _____ pages

6. Roger's lunch bag has 16 grapes and an apple. Rosa's lunch bag has 14 grapes and an orange. How many grapes do they have together?

   _____ grapes

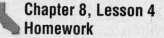
Hands On: Add 2-Digit Numbers in Different Ways

CA Standards
KEY NS 2.2, MR 1.2

Fill in the boxes. Use counters or secret code cards.

	Show both numbers.	Add the ones. How many tens and ones are there?	Do you need to regroup?	What is the sum?
1.	18 + 16	__2__ tens __14__ ones	Yes No	34
2.	32 + 27	_____ tens _____ ones	Yes No	
3.	75 + 5	_____ tens _____ ones	Yes No	
4.	68 + 9	_____ tens _____ ones	Yes No	

5. Add 15 peanuts and 32 peanuts. Use counters and secret code cards to check your answer.

_____ peanuts

Spiral Review   (Chapter 7, Lesson 1) **KEY** NS 5.1, NS 5.0

6. Ruth has 2 dimes. She gives them to Larry because she owes him 12¢. How much change does she get back?

_____ cents

7. John buys something for 87¢ and pays for it with a $1. Count on from the price to get the change. How much change does John get?

_____

Hands On: Add 2-Digit Numbers in Different Ways

CA Standards
KEY NS 2.2, MR 1.2

Solve.

1. Melanie has 12 pennies and Chantal has 13 pennies. Use secret code cards to see how much money they have together.

_____ pennies

2. Roger runs for 18 minutes and jogs for 10 minutes. How many minutes does Roger exercise? Use counters to solve.

_____ minutes

3. Elise read 18 pages in her book last night, and she will read 19 more pages tonight. Use secret code cards to find how many pages she read in both nights.

_____ pages

4. Renga wrote thank you notes to his relatives. He wrote 15 in the morning and 17 in the afternoon. Use counters to find how many he wrote all together.

_____ notes

5. Raoul bought a bag of 40 peanuts. He ate 23 of them at the movie. How many did he have left?

_____ peanuts

6. Marla has three secret code cards. The first shows a 37. The second card has the first box blanked out, and the second box is a 2. The two code cards together equal the third card, which is 59. What is the missing number?

_____

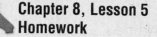
Too Much Information

CA Standard
AF 1.2

> Sometimes a problem has more information than you need.

**Cross out any information you do not need. Then
solve. Explain your answers to a family member.**

1. There are 12 children at field day. Later, 11 children join them.
   Then 5 parents come to watch. How many children are at field day?

   _23_ children

2. Charles watered 16 tulips and 15 roses. Jill watered 10 tulips. How
   many tulips were watered?

   _____ tulips

3. Elena washes 16 carrots and 10 apples in the morning. Javier washes
   24 carrots in the afternoon. How many carrots were washed?

   _____ carrots

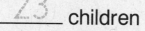 **Spiral Review** (Chapter 7, Lesson 1) **KEYS** NS 5.1, NS 5.0

4. Marguerite has 2 quarters, 3 dimes, 1 nickel, and 2 pennies. How
   much money does she have?

   _____

Too Much Information

Solve.

1. Mike has 14 pairs of socks and a kitten that likes to play with them. Louis has 12 pairs of socks. How many pairs of socks do they have together?

   _____ pairs of socks

2. Ellen wrote 13 thank you notes for her birthday presents. Susan wrote 10 thank you notes. How many thank you notes did they write in all?

   _____ thank you notes

3. The Waterpark sold 40 children's tickets for the Chutes and Splash Ride. It also sold 25 children's tickets for Wave Pool. The same day, it sold 28 adult tickets for the Wave Pool. How many children's tickets did it sell in all?

   _____ children's tickets

4. The grocery store sold 46 pounds of MacIntosh apples, 28 pounds of Fuji apples, and 50 pounds of string beans. How many pounds of apples did it sell all together?

   _____ pounds

5. Ramone has $23 in paper money and $1.25 in change. Martha has $14 in paper money and $0.88 in change. How much do they have together in paper money?

   _____ dollars

6. The class ran a recycling drive over two weeks. The first week they collected 25 pounds of paper and 12 pounds of plastic. The second week they collected 43 pounds of glass and 27 pounds of paper. How many pounds of paper did they collect in all?

   _____ pounds

Hands On: Add Using a Hundred Chart

**Use the hundred chart. Add.
Find 44 + 30.**

First find 44 on the hundred chart. Then count on by tens to add 30. Count by tens by moving down the rows.

$44 + 30 = \underline{74}$

1	2	3	4	5	6	7	8	9	10
11	12	13	14	15	16	17	18	19	20
21	22	23	24	25	26	27	28	29	30
31	32	33	34	35	36	37	38	39	40
41	42	43	44	45	46	47	48	49	50
51	52	53	54	55	56	57	58	59	60
61	62	63	64	65	66	67	68	69	70
71	72	73	74	75	76	77	78	79	80
81	82	83	84	85	86	87	88	89	90
91	92	93	94	95	96	97	98	99	100

Use the hundred chart. Add.

1. $18 + 30 =$ ___   2. $10 + 49 =$ ___   3. $40 + 17 =$ ___

4. 34
   $+ 40$

5. 20
   $+ 13$

6. 50
   $+ 20$

Spiral Review (Chapter 8, Lesson 1) **NS 2.3, KEY NS 2.2**

7. If you add 3 tens and 4 tens, what is the sum?

8. Rolf has 5 dimes, and Manuel gives him 3 more. How much money does he have?

Hands On: Add Using a Hundred Chart

CA Standard
KEY NS 2.2

Solve using a hundred chart.

1. Marla has 10 pencils and buys 10 more. How many pencils does she have?

   _____ pencils

2. Mai practiced ballet for 12 minutes and practiced tap for ten minutes more. How long did she practice?

   _____ minutes

3. Oscar has 25 stickers in his book and is given a sheet of 30 more. How many stickers does he have?

   _____ stickers

4. Roberto has 37 baseball trading cards. He then buys 3 packs more and each pack has 10 cards. How many cards does he have?

   _____ trading cards

5. Annabel had 20 pages filled out in her scrapbook. 8 more friends fill out one page each. How many pages does she have filled out now?

   _____ pages

6. The pet shop had 23 goldfish in the tank. A new shipment came in and 11 more goldfish were added. How many are there in the tank?

   _____ fish

Add Using a Place-Value Chart

CA Standards
KEY NS 2.2, NS 2.0

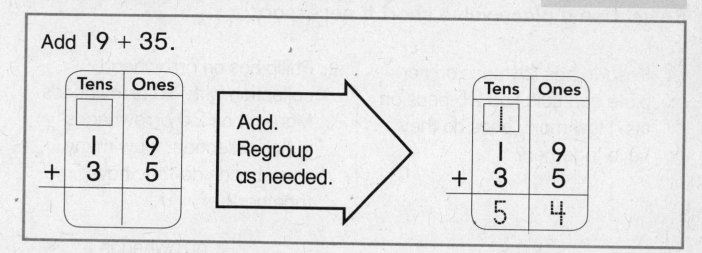

Add 19 + 35.

Add. Record your work.

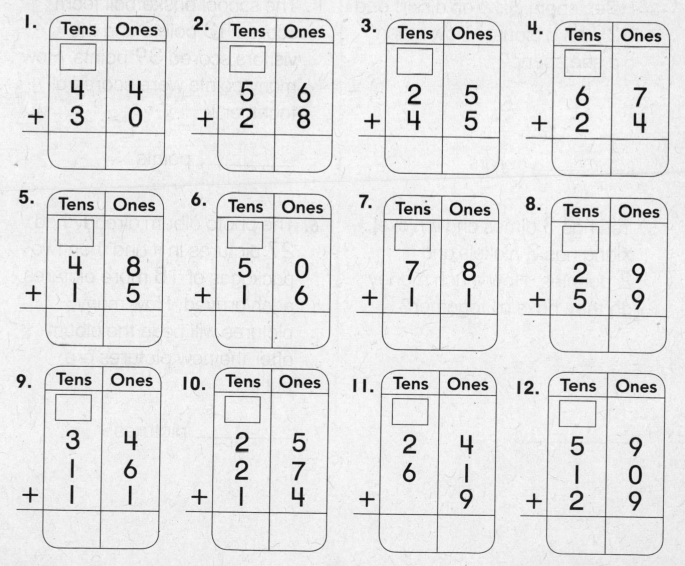

Add Using a Place-Value Chart

CA Standards
KEY NS 2.2, NS 2.0

Solve. Use a place-value chart if necessary.

1. Rosario has 24 peas on her plate and Luis had 25 peas on his. How many peas do they have together?

_____ peas

2. Philip has an arrowhead collection with 30 arrowheads. Marilyn has 20 arrowheads in her collection. How many arrowheads do they have together?

_____ arrowheads

3. Helen spent $32 on a skirt and $29 on a blouse. How much did she spend?

_____ dollars

4. The school basketball team scored 43 points and the visitors scored 39 points. How many points were scored all together?

_____ points

5. Yen has 3 dimes and a nickel. Xiang has 3 nickels and 2 pennies. How much money do they have all together?

_____ ¢

6. The photo album already had 27 pictures in it and then two packages of 18 more pictures each arrived. How many pictures will be in the album after the new pictures are put in?

_____ pictures

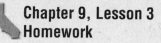
Practice Regrouping 10 to 14

CA Standard
KEY NS 2.2

If there are 10 or more ones, you need to regroup.

Solve. Use 10 attached 🖇 to show tens.

Use single 🖇 to show ones.

	Show both numbers.	Add the ones. How many tens and ones are there?	Do you need to regroup?	What is the sum?
1.	16 + 8	_____ ten _____ ones	Yes No	
2.	39 + 4	_____ tens _____ ones	Yes No	
3.	24 + 5	_____ tens _____ ones	Yes No	

4. Place 29 beans in rows of 10, 10, and 9. Then add 5 more beans. How many beans do you have in all? Regroup to solve.

_____ beans

Spiral Review   (Chapter 8, Lesson 3) **KEY NS 2.2**

5. $14 + 9 =$ _____

6. $26 + 29 =$ _____

7. $13 + 38 =$ _____

8. $22 + 12 =$ _____

Practice Regrouping 10 to 14

CA Standard
KEY NS 2.2

Solve.

1. Jake has 23 pennies. Janice has 24 pennies. They stack the pennies in groups of 10. How many stacks of 10 are there?

_____ stacks

2. Oscar has 15 pairs of socks. Orlando also has 15 pairs of socks. How many pairs do they have together?

_____ pairs

3. Ruth ran for 25 minutes on Monday. She ran for 27 minutes on Tuesday. How many minutes did she run for the two days?

_____ minutes

4. Alexei swam 18 laps and took a rest. He then swam 15 laps more. How many laps did he swim?

_____ laps

5. Rochelle went to Cape Cod when she was 18. She went there again when she was 31. How many years passed between her first and second visits?

_____ years

6. Michael's first toss of the discus went 38 feet. After he practiced a lot, he was able to toss it 72 feet. How many feet did his toss improve?

_____ feet

Practice Regrouping 15 to 18

CA Standard
KEY NS 2.2

Use these steps to add two-digit numbers with regrouping.		
Step ❶ Add the ones.	**Step ❷ Regroup 10 ones as 1 ten.**	**Step ❸ Add the tens.**

Use 10 attached 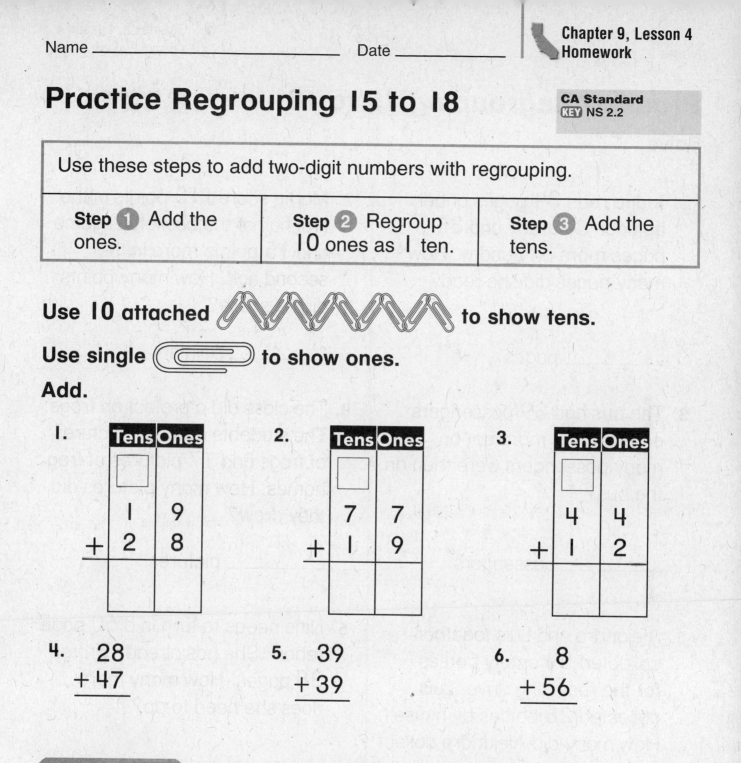 to show tens.

Use single ⬭ to show ones.

Add.

1.

Tens	Ones
1	9
+ 2	8

2.

Tens	Ones
7	7
+ 1	9

3.

Tens	Ones
4	4
+ 1	2

4. 28
   + 47
   _____

5. 39
   + 39
   _____

6.   8
   + 56
   _____

Spiral Review (Chapter 8, Lesson 4) **KEY NS 2.2, MR 1.2**

7. Use secret code cards or other means to add 23 and 42. _____

8. Maurice is picking tomatoes from his garden. Yesterday, he picked 12 tomatoes. Today he picked 14 more. How many tomatoes did he pick?

_____

Practice Regrouping 15 to 18

CA Standard
KEY NS 2.2

Solve.

1. Indira read 34 pages of her book on Saturday and 35 pages more on Sunday. How many pages did she read?

_____ pages

2. Martin scored 13 points in the first half of the basketball game and 15 points more in the second half. How many points did he score?

_____ points

3. The bus had 39 passengers and then 19 more got on. How many passengers were then on the bus?

_____ passengers

4. The class did a project on frogs. The students drew 18 pictures of frogs and 17 pictures of frog homes. How many pictures did they draw?

_____ pictures

5. Alejandro and Luis together collected 54 empty bottles for the recycling drive. Luis collected 28 bottles by himself. How many did Alejandro collect by himself?

_____ bottles

6. Nina needs to turn in a 60 page report. She has already written 38 pages. How many more does she need to do?

_____ pages

Guess and Check

CA Standard
KEY NS 2.2, MR 2.0

Use Guess and Check to solve.

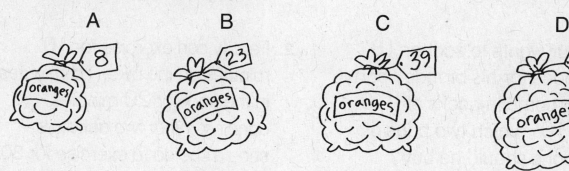

A · 8 B · 23 C · 39 D · 57

1. Steven buys 47 oranges. Which two
   bags does he buy?

   _____ and _____

2. The coach hands out 65 oranges as snacks.

   Which two bags does he use to hand out oranges?

   _____ and _____

3. Manuel needs 96 oranges for his family party.

   Which two bags should he get?

   _____ and _____

Spiral Review   (Chapter 8, Lesson 5) **SDAP 1.4, AF 1.2**

4. Marcel has 25 comic books, 14 story books, 2 dogs, and a toy ship.

   How many books does Marcel have? _____ books

5. Judy had a birthday party and invited 12 friends. She also had
   a party with her family, and 13 relatives came. How many
   people came to her parties?

   _____ people

Guess and Check

CA Standards
KEY NS 2.2, MR 2.0

Solve.

1. Arthur wants to scatter 18 balloons for his birthday party. They come in packs of 4, 8, and 10. Which two bags of balloons should he buy?

   _____

2. Felicity can exercise for 10 minutes on the bike, 18 minutes in the pool, or 20 minutes dancing. What two activities should she do to exercise for 30 minutes?

   _____

3. Laundry detergent comes in bottles holding 12 ounces, 32 ounces, 60 ounces, and 100 ounces. What should you buy to have 72 ounces?

   _____

4. Stamps come in sheets of 8, 20, 50, or 100 stamps. What do you buy in order to mail 58 letters?

   _____

5. Carlos needs carrots. The store has bags with either 2 pounds or 5 pounds. What should he buy in order to get 8 pounds of carrots?

   _____

6. The store sells flour in 1-lb, 5-lb, and 10-lb bags. What is the fewest number of bags to buy to get 25 lb of flour?

   _____

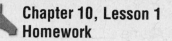
Hands On: Different Ways to Add

CA Standards
KEY NS 2.2, MR 1.0

Here are different ways to add: mental math,
hundred chart, place-value blocks, and paper and pencil.
The better way to add is circled.

52 + 29
(paper and pencil) mental math

25 + 10
hundred chart (mental math)

75 + 38
(hundred chart) mental math

40 + 8
hundred chart (place-value blocks)

Choose a way to add. Add. Explain the way you find the sum.

1. 38 + 49   Sum _____

_____
_____
_____

2. 25 + 30   Sum _____

_____
_____
_____

3. 77 + 16   Sum _____

_____
_____
_____

4. 30 + 7   Sum _____

_____
_____
_____

Spiral Review   (Chapter 9, Lesson 1) **KEY** NS 2.2

5. Use the hundred chart to add 30 to 47. _____

6. What was added to 26 if the answer is 76? _____

Use with text pp. 189–190

Hands On: Different Ways to Add

CA Standards
KEY NS 2.2, MR 1.0

Solve. Use any method you wish.

1. Martha has 20 large paper plates and 20 small paper plates. How many plates does she have?

_____ plates

2. Sunil washed 14 big cars and 10 small cars for the fundraiser. How many cars did he wash?

_____ cars

3. Esther baked 24 big cookies and 36 small cookies for the PTA meeting. How many cookies did she bake?

_____ cookies

4. The baseball team has 28 players and the football team has 44 players. How many players are there on the two teams?

_____ players

5. Roger received 44 suggestions from Arnold and Mary. Arnold sent in 18 suggestions. How many suggestions did Mary send?

_____ suggestions

6. 34 children are playing on the field. 17 are playing with Frisbees and the rest are playing with a soccer ball. How many children are playing with the soccer ball?

_____ children

Estimate Sums

CA Standards
NS 6.0, NS 2.0

Use a number line to estimate the sum of 22 and 37.
Round each addend to the nearest ten.

20 21 22 23 24 25 26 27 28 29 30 31 32 33 34 35 36 37 38 39 40

Solution: ___20___ + ___40___ = ___60___

Use the number lines to round each addend to the nearest ten.
Estimate the sum.

10 11 12 13 14 15 16 17 18 19 20 21 22 23 24 25 26 27 28 29 30

30 31 32 33 34 35 36 37 38 39 40 41 42 43 44 45 46 47 48 49 50

1. $18 + 23$

____ + ____ = ____

2. $41 + 17$

____ + ____ = ____

3. $42 + 28$

____ + ____ = ____

4. $50 + 35$

____ + ____ = ____

Spiral Review (Chapter 9, Lesson 2) **KEY** NS 2.2, NS 2.0

5. $28 + 45 =$

6. $77 + 12 =$

7. $36 + 56 =$

8. $14 + 19 =$

Tens	Ones
+	

Tens	Ones
+	

Tens	Ones
+	

Tens	Ones
+	

Use with text pp. 191–192

Estimate Sums

CA Standards
NS 6.0, NS 2.0

Solve.

1. The first section took 30 minutes to eat their lunch. The second section took 20 minutes. About how much time was spent eating lunch?

   _____ minutes

2. Lin has 40 pictures of policemen, and 30 pictures of firemen. About how many pictures does he have?

   _____ pictures

3. Gloria and David played Ring Toss. Gloria scored 45 points and David scored 42. Estimate their total score.

   About _____ points

4. Marcel planted 18 bean plants and 26 tomato plants. About how many plants did he plant?

   About _____ plants

5. Fawza has 12 pens, 21 pencils, and 18 markers. About how many writing tools does she have?

   About _____ writing tools

6. Marsha has 14 picture postcards, 12 plain postcards, and 24 sheets of stationary. About how many postcards does she have?

   About _____ postcards

Name _____ Date _____

Line Up Digits to Add

CA Standard
KEY NS 2.2

You can rewrite addends in vertical form.
Place the first addend on top and the
second addend on the bottom.

$29 + 67 =$

Tens	Ones
1	
2	9
6	7
+ 9	6

Remember to line up the ones and tens.

Rewrite the addends. Add.

1. $15 + 36 =$ 2. $9 + 47 =$ 3. $73 + 14 =$ 4. $25 + 25 =$

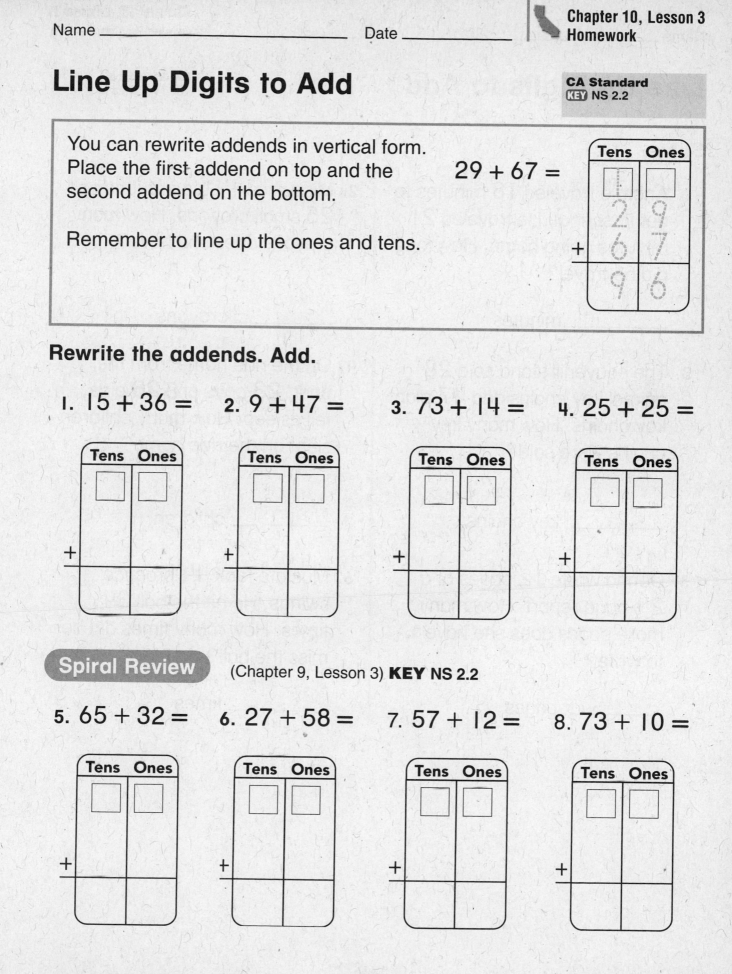

Spiral Review (Chapter 9, Lesson 3) **KEY** NS 2.2

5. $65 + 32 =$ 6. $27 + 58 =$ 7. $57 + 12 =$ 8. $73 + 10 =$

Use with text pp. 193–194

Line Up Digits to Add

CA Standard
KEY NS 2.2

Solve.

1. Anatole traveled 18 minutes to get to school. He traveled 21 minutes going home. How long did he travel?

_____ minutes

2. Missy has 14 big crayons and 25 small crayons. How many crayons does she have?

_____ crayons

3. The souvenir stand sold 28 animal key chains and 47 plant key chains. How many key chains were sold?

_____ key chains

4. On the ride home from the park, 23 boys and 28 girls fell asleep. How many children slept on the ride home?

_____ children

5. Donna wrote 12 pages of a 24-page report. How many more pages does she have to write?

_____ pages

6. Mustafa took 44 practice swings. He hit the ball 34 times. How many times did he miss the ball?

_____ times

Name ____________________ Date ____________

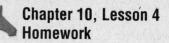

Add Money

CA Standards
KEY NS 2.2, NS 5.0

You can add money the same way you add numbers.

Add.		Rewrite the numbers. Then add.	Rewrite the numbers. Then add.
		32¢ + 49¢	17¢ + 59¢
40¢ + 40¢ 80¢	1 56¢ + 16¢ 72¢	1 32¢ + 49¢ 81¢	1 17¢ + 59¢ 76¢

Add.

1. 50¢ + 16¢
2. 67¢ + 24¢
3. 41¢ + 5¢
4. 35¢ + 11¢
5. 79¢ + 14¢
6. 51¢ + 38¢
7. 78¢ + 11¢
8. 19¢ + 79¢

Spiral Review (Chapter 9, Lesson 4) **KEY NS 2.2**

9. 27 + 68
10. 87 + 9
11. 34 + 16
12. 35 + 44

Add Money

CA Standards
KEY NS 2.2, NS 5.0

Solve.

1. Moira has 10 pennies and Elise has 15 pennies. How many pennies do they have together?

   _____ pennies

2. Peter has 25¢. He finds a quarter in his pocket. How much money does he now have?

   _____

3. Rudy puts 38¢ in his bank on Monday. On Friday, he puts 43¢ into his bank. How much money did Rudy put into his bank?

   _____

4. Jeff and Dan are saving their money together. Jeff puts 44¢ into the piggy bank. Dan puts in 38¢. How much money is in the piggy bank?

   _____

5. Craig has 69¢. His sister lends him a quarter and 4 pennies. How much money does Craig have?

   _____

6. Rosanna spent $15 on a skirt. She received $35 in change. How much money did she give the clerk?

   _____

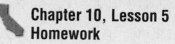
Add Three 2-Digit Numbers

CA Standards
KEY AF 1.1, NS 2.0

You can use two ways to add three 2-digit numbers.

Make a ten.	Use a fact you know.
$\begin{array}{r} 26 \\ +34 \\ +11 \\ \hline 71 \end{array}$ >6 + 4 = 10	$\begin{array}{r} 54 \\ 14 \\ +5 \\ \hline 73 \end{array}$ >4 + 4 = 8

Add.

1. $\begin{array}{r} 53 \\ 33 \\ +2 \\ \hline \end{array}$
2. $\begin{array}{r} 44 \\ 18 \\ +10 \\ \hline \end{array}$
3. $\begin{array}{r} 9 \\ 51 \\ +26 \\ \hline \end{array}$
4. $\begin{array}{r} 16 \\ 26 \\ +20 \\ \hline \end{array}$
5. $\begin{array}{r} 36 \\ 11 \\ +34 \\ \hline \end{array}$

6. $\begin{array}{r} 13 \\ 40 \\ +9 \\ \hline \end{array}$
7. $\begin{array}{r} 11 \\ 4 \\ +50 \\ \hline \end{array}$
8. $\begin{array}{r} 32 \\ 28 \\ +2 \\ \hline \end{array}$
9. $\begin{array}{r} 17 \\ 13 \\ +25 \\ \hline \end{array}$
10. $\begin{array}{r} 20 \\ 13 \\ +13 \\ \hline \end{array}$

Spiral Review (Chapter 9, Lesson 5) **KEY NS 2.2, MR 2.0**

11. Marlene has 14 crayons, Rita has 24 crayons, and Ari has 16 crayons. Two of them work together and have 30 crayons. Which two work together?

_____

12. The museum has 18 lizards, 22 mice, and 14 rats. It gets 40 new cages. Which animals get to go in the new cages?

_____

Name _____ Date _____

Add Three 2-Digit Numbers

Solve.

1. The music store has 10 trumpets, 20 guitars, and 5 violins. How many instruments does the store have?

_____ instruments

2. Manny has 10 toy cars, 2 toy trucks, and 8 toy fire engines. How many toy vehicles does Manny have?

_____ vehicles

3. The toy store sold 22 bikes, 18 scooters, and 24 skateboards. How many toys did the store sell?

_____ toys

4. The fruit store sold 14 pounds of apples, 22 pounds of oranges, and 16 pounds of bananas. How many pounds of fruit were sold?

_____ pounds

5. Monica read 18 novels, 17 biographies, 14 history books, and 4 newspapers. How many books did Monica read?

_____ books

6. The recycling drive collected 42 pounds of glass, 12 pounds of aluminum, 8 pounds of cardboard, and 37 pounds of paper. How many pounds were recycled?

_____ pounds

Comparison Problems

CA Standards
KEY NS 2.2, AF 1.3

Devon needs new shin guards and cleats. How much money does he need?

What do you know?

The shin guards cost _35¢_.

The cleats cost _63¢_.

Item	Price
Shin guards	35¢
Cleats	63¢
Soccer Ball	37¢
Uniform	46¢

Write the parts you know in the comparison bars.

Write a number sentence.

Then solve.

_35¢_ + _63¢_ = _98¢_

Shin guards	Cleats
35¢	63¢
98¢	

Solution: Devon needs _98¢_ to buy the items.

Use the table above to solve.

1. Samantha wants to buy a new uniform and shin guards.
   How much money does she need? _____

2. Rohit buys a uniform and a soccer ball.
   How much does he spend? _____

Spiral Review (Chapter 9, Lesson 5) **KEY AF 1.1, NS 2.0**

3. There are 25 players on Coach Ross' team. He can buy new jerseys in bags of 10, 12, or 15. Which bags does he buy for his team?

   _____ and _____

4. Anneke buys 32 jerseys. Which 3 bags does she buy?

   _____ _____ and _____

Comparison Problems

CA Standards
KEY NS 2.2, AF 1.3

Solve.

1. Estelle sees a hat for 37¢ and a hat for 59¢. How much money does she need to buy both hats?

   _____ ¢

2. Randall scored 18 points in the basketball game. Courtney scored 22 points. How many points did they score in all?

   _____ points

3. Robert's train set is 33 inches long. Greg's is 28 inches long. If the boys put their train sets together, how long would they be?

   _____ inches

4. Gary ran the first lap of the relay in 26 seconds. Michael ran the second lap in 28 seconds. What was their total time?

   _____ seconds

5. Jane records the number of animals that the Nature Club saw. They saw 8 blackbirds, 5 blue jays, and 12 squirrels. How many animals does Jane record?

   _____ animals

6. John and Jim were on team 1. Susie and Sally were on team 2. John scored 8 points and Jim scored 9. Susie scored 12 points and Sally scored 6. Which team scored more points?

   _____

Hands On: Subtract Tens

When you subtract tens, think of subtraction fact.

$50 - 20 =$

$5 - 2 = \underline{3}$

$5 \text{ tens} - 2 \text{ tens} = \underline{3} \text{ tens}$

$50 - 20 = \underline{30}$

Complete the subtraction sentences.
Use a basic fact to help.

1. $8 \text{ tens} - 5 \text{ tens} = \underline{\quad} \text{ tens}$ 2. $5 \text{ tens} - 4 \text{ tens} = \underline{\quad} \text{ ten}$

   $\underline{\quad} - \underline{\quad} = \underline{\quad}$ $\underline{\quad} - \underline{\quad} = \underline{\quad}$

3. $6 \text{ tens} - 4 \text{ tens} = \underline{\quad} \text{ tens}$ 4. $7 \text{ tens} - 2 \text{ tens} = \underline{\quad} \text{ tens}$

   $\underline{\quad} - \underline{\quad} = \underline{\quad}$ $\underline{\quad} - \underline{\quad} = \underline{\quad}$

5. $7 \text{ tens} - 4 \text{ tens} = \underline{\quad} \text{ tens}$ 6. $6 \text{ tens} - 5 \text{ tens} = \underline{\quad} \text{ tens}$

   $\underline{\quad} - \underline{\quad} = \underline{\quad}$ $\underline{\quad} - \underline{\quad} = \underline{\quad}$

Spiral Review (Chapter 10, Lesson 1) **KEY** NS 2.2, MR 1.0

7. Choose a way to add and add $14 + 20$.

   mental math
   paper and pencil

8. Choose a way to add and add $35 + 47$.

   mental math
   paper and pencil

Hands On: Subtract Tens

CA Standard
KEY NS 2.2, MR 1.2

Solve. Use counters if necessary.

1. There are 60 red markers in the storage room. Mrs. Hanley takes 20 of them. How many are left?

   _____ markers

2. Maria bought a box of 40 thank you cards. She sent out 20 of them. How many are left?

   _____ cards

3. A store has 8 boxes each of red and black pencils. Each box has ten pencils. 4 boxes of red pencils and 6 boxes of black pencils are sold. How many pencils are left?

   _____ pencils

4. Frank was given 40 posters to hand out. He gave one to each person in his class. If his class has 10 people besides him, how many posters does Frank have left?

   _____ posters

5. Mr. Mathias has a book with 80 stickers. He teaches a class with 20 students. He gives each student 2 stickers. How many stickers does he have left?

   _____ stickers

6. Francesca baked 100 rolls for the picnic. 45 people came and each took 2 rolls. How many rolls were left?

   _____ rolls

Hands On: Subtract 2-Digit Numbers

CA Standards
KEY NS 2.2, MR 1.2

Model and draw to subtract. Find each difference.

1. $63 - 31 =$	2. $24 - 12 =$	3. $49 - 27 =$
4. $36 - 16 =$	5. $75 - 64 =$	6. $58 - 14 =$

Spiral Review (Chapter 10, Lesson 2) **NS 6.0, NS 2.0**

Round each addend to the nearest ten. Estimate the sum.

7. $44 + 32$ ____ + ____ = ____   8. $28 + 11$ ____ + ____ = ____

9. $56 + 29$ ____ + ____ = ____   10. $43 + 19$ ____ + ____ = ____

Hands On: Subtract 2-Digit Numbers

CA Standards
KEY NS 2.2, MR 1.1

Solve. Use counters if necessary.

1. John bought 45 tickets at the fair. He used 15 for the merry-go-round. How many tickets did he have left?

   _____ tickets

2. Rosa has a collection of 30 barrettes. She lends 10 to her sister. How many barrettes does she have left?

   _____ barrettes

3. Louis has 67¢ in his pocket. He gives 26¢ to his friend Moe. How much money does Louis have left?

   _____ ¢

4. The football team was 86 yards away from the goal. The next play they got 24 yards closer. How far were they from the goal?

   _____ yards

5. Millie has 45 minutes to complete her homework and 15 minutes to get ready for bed. She works on history for 22 minutes. How much time does she have left for homework?

   _____ minutes

6. A block of ice weighed 50 pounds. It was left out in the sun for an hour and then weighed 35 pounds. How much weight did it lose?

   _____ pounds

Hands On: Subtract 2-Digit Numbers With Regrouping

CA Standards
KEY NS 2.2, MR 2.1

Find 31 – 5.

Show the greater number.	Subtract the smaller number.	Do you need to regroup?	How many tens and ones are left?	What is the difference?
31	5	Yes (circled) / No	2 tens / 6 ones	26

Solution: 31 – 5 = 26

1. 43 – 7 =

_____ tens _____ ones =

_____

2. 50 – 4 =

_____ tens _____ ones =

_____

3. 71 – 24 =

_____ tens _____ ones =

_____

4. 85 – 75 =

_____ tens _____ ones =

_____

5. 74 – 28 =

_____ tens _____ ones =

_____

6. 42 – 9 =

_____ tens _____ ones =

_____

7. 72 – 54 =

_____ tens _____ ones =

_____

8. 14 – 8 =

_____ tens _____ ones =

_____

Spiral Review (Chapter 10, Lesson 3) **KEY NS 2.2**

9. 34 + 27 = _____

10. 48 + 39 = _____

Use with text pp. 219–220

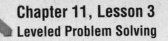
Hands On: Subtract 2-Digit Numbers With Regrouping

CA Standards
KEY NS 2.2, MR 2.1

Solve.

1. Greta buys 6 packs of 10 sheets of notepaper. Marta has the same number of sheets, but 20 of them are loose. How many packs does Marta have?

_____ packs

2. Markers come packed 10 to a box. Jake gets 5 boxes. Jared has the same number of markers, but only 3 boxes. How many loose markers does Jared have?

_____ markers

3. Jamal rode his bike for 45 minutes on Wednesday and only 28 minutes on Thursday. How many minutes more did he ride on Wednesday?

_____ minutes

4. The lunchroom staff made 64 tuna sandwiches. They served 38 of them. How many were left?

_____ sandwiches

5. Joy gave 12 roses to Marsha. She gave another 12 roses to Lucy. She had 6 left. How many roses did she start with?

_____ roses

6. Ricky shared his grapes with Mario and his carrots with Oscar. If Mario got 18 grapes and Ricky ate 19, how may grapes did Ricky start with?

_____ grapes

Use with text pp. 219–220

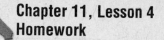
Make a Table

CA Standards
KEY NS 2.2, AF 1.3

You can use information in a table to solve
a problem.

The second grade planted trees
for Earth Day.

This table shows how many
trees they planted.

**Use the table to solve each
problem. Explain your answers
to a family member.**

Trees	Number Planted
Oak trees	56
Maple trees	17
Apple trees	49
Birch trees	38

1. How many oak and maple trees
   were planted?

   _____ oak and maple trees

2. How many more apple trees
   than maple trees were planted?

   _____ more apple trees

3. How many fewer apple trees
   than oak trees were planted?

   _____ fewer apple trees

4. How many maple and birch
   trees were planted?

   _____ maple and birch trees

Spiral Review (Chapter 10, Lesson 4) **KEY** NS 2.2, NS 5.0

5. Ruth has 2 dimes and 6 pennies.
   She finds a quarter in her pocket.
   How much money does she have? _____

6. John has 84¢ and he buys a pencil for 39¢.
   How much money does he have left? _____

Make a Table

Solve using the table.

CA Standards
KEY NS 2.2, AF 1.3

The Math Club is going on a club trip. Members had a choice of four places to go. The table shows how many voted for each place.

Place to visit	Votes
Aquarium	32
Museum	46
Planet show	27
Zoo	29

1. Which got more votes, the aquarium or the museum?

   _____

2. How many votes were there for either the aquarium or the museum?

   _____ votes

3. How many more votes were for the museum than for the aquarium?

   _____ votes

4. How many more votes were for the museum than for the zoo?

   _____ votes

5. Which kind of trip was more popular, a trip to see live animals or a trip to either the museum or the planet show? By how many votes?

   _____

   _____

   _____

6. If each club member could vote for two trips, how many club members are there?

   _____ members

Hands on: Subtract Using a Hundred Chart

CA Standards
KEY NS 2.2, MR 1.2

You can use a hundred chart to help you subtract.

Find 76 – 30.

First find **76** on the hundred chart.
Then move up **3** rows to subtract **30**.

76 – 30 = 46

1	2	3	4	5	6	7	8	9	10
11	12	13	14	15	16	17	18	19	20
21	22	23	24	25	26	27	28	29	30
31	32	33	34	35	36	37	38	39	40
41	42	43	44	45	46	47	48	49	50
51	52	53	54	55	56	57	58	59	60
61	62	63	64	65	66	67	68	69	70
71	72	73	74	75	76	77	78	79	80
81	82	83	84	85	86	87	88	89	90
91	92	93	94	95	96	97	98	99	100

Use the hundred chart.
Subtract.

1. 38 – 20 = ____

2. 66 – 40 = ____

3. 95 – 40 = ____

4. 26 – 10 = ____

5. 77
  –20

6. 83
  –50

7. 46
  –10

8. 80
  –70

Spiral Review (Chapter 11, Lesson 1) **KEY NS 2.2, MR 1.2**

9. What is 50 – 20?

_____

10. What is 80 – 40?

_____

Name _____   Date _____

Hands on: Subtract Using a Hundred Chart

CA Standards
KEY NS 2.2, MR 1.2

Bess, Jonah, Rona, and Alvin use a hundred chart to play a board game. Solve the problems.

1	2	3	4	5	6	7	8	9	10
11	12	13	14	15	16	17	18	19	20
21	22	23	24	25	26	27	28	29	30
31	32	33	34	35	36	37	38	39	40
41	42	43	44	45	46	47	48	49	50
51	52	53	54	55	56	57	58	59	60
61	62	63	64	65	66	67	68	69	70
71	72	73	74	75	76	77	78	79	80
81	82	83	84	85	86	87	88	89	90
91	92	93	94	95	96	97	98	99	100

1. Jonah puts his marker on number 60. He picks a game card that reads, "You lose 30 points." On what number should he put his marker?

_____

2. Bess has her marker on number 70. Her game card reads, "You lose 40 points." On what number should Bess put her marker?

_____

3. Rona puts her marker on number 54. She picks a game card that reads, "You lose 10 points." Where should she put her marker?

_____

4. Alvin's marker is on number 96. His game card reads, "You lose 60 points." On what number should Alvin put his marker?

_____

5. Martin wants to practice piano for 45 minutes. He has been practicing for 10 minutes already. How much practice time does he have left?

_____ minutes

6. Marge has 85¢ in her purse. She buys 3 pieces of gum, which cost 10¢ each. How much money does she have left?

_____ ¢

Name _____ Date _____

Hands On: Subtract Using a Place-Value Chart

CA Standards
KEY NS 2.2, MR 1.2

You can regroup numbers to subtract one-digit numbers from two-digit numbers.

Subtract: 44 – 6

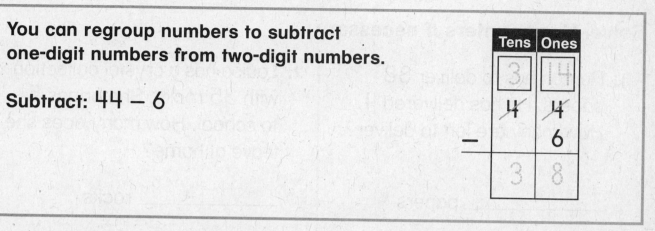

Tens	Ones
3	14
4	4
–	6
3	8

Subtract. Record each step.

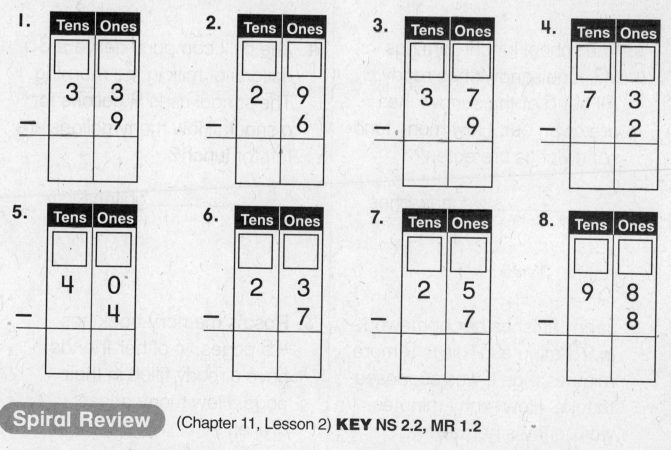

1.
Tens	Ones
3	3
–	9

2.
Tens	Ones
2	9
–	6

3.
Tens	Ones
3	7
–	9

4.
Tens	Ones
7	3
–	2

5.
Tens	Ones
4	0
–	4

6.
Tens	Ones
2	3
–	7

7.
Tens	Ones
2	5
–	7

8.
Tens	Ones
9	8
–	8

Spiral Review (Chapter 11, Lesson 2) **KEY** NS 2.2, MR 1.2

9. Mary had 34 guppies. 21 died. How many were left?

_____ guppies

10. Raoul wanted to hike 25 miles. He went 14 miles and took a rest. How many miles did he have left? _____ miles

Use with text pp. 231–232

Hands On: Subtract Using a Place-Value Chart

CA Standards
KEY NS 2.2, MR 1.2

Solve. Use counters if necessary.

1. Ramon has to deliver 38 papers. He has delivered 4. How many are left to deliver?

_____ papers

2. Louisa has a crystal collection with 35 rocks. She brings 5 to school. How many does she leave at home?

_____ rocks

3. The school lunchroom has 97 tuna sandwiches ready. All but 6 of the sandwiches are given out. How many tuna sandwiches are eaten?

_____ sandwiches

4. The milk company delivers 35 gallons of milk in the morning. The school uses 9 gallons for a snack. How many gallons are left for lunch?

_____ gallons

5. Jenny finishes her homework in 48 minutes. This is 9 more minutes than it was supposed to take. How many minutes was Jenny's homework supposed to take?

_____ minutes

6. Rosa's memory book has 45 pages. 7 of her friends have already filled in their page. How many pages are left?

_____ pages

Name _____ Date _____

Practice Regrouping with 10 to 14

CA Standards
KEY NS 2.2, NS 2.0

Find 33−5.

Step 1 Show 33.

3 tens 3 ones

Step 2 Regroup one ten as ten ones.

2 tens 13 ones

Step 3 Subtract 5.

2 tens 8 ones

Solution: 33 − 5 = ___28___

		Do you need to regroup to subtract?		Subtract the ones. How many tens and ones are left?	What is the difference?
1.	34 − 6	Yes	No	_____ tens _____ ones	_____
2.	44 − 3	Yes	No	_____ tens _____ ones	_____
3.	22 − 5	Yes	No	_____ tens _____ ones	_____
4.	31 − 9	Yes	No	_____ tens _____ ones	_____
5.	42 − 4	Yes	No	_____ tens _____ ones	_____

Spiral Review (Chapter 11, Lesson 3) **KEY NS 2.2, MR 2.1**

6. Waldo got a 78 on his first test and a 94 on his second test. How many points did he improve?

_____ points

7. The Scoutmaster packed 47 sandwiches for lunch. The Scouts ate 29 of them. How many sandwiches were left?

_____ sandwiches

Use with text pp. 233–234

Practice Regrouping with 10 to 14

Solve.

1. Marcy has 50¢ in her bank. She gives 20¢ to her little sister. How much money does she have left?

   _____

2. Tyrone collected 44 oak and maple leaves for his science project. 12 were oak leaves. How many were maple leaves?

   _____ leaves

3. Chan has 32 marbles. He gives 14 red marbles to his friend Luke. How many marbles does Chan have left?

   _____ marbles

4. Lita is reading a book that is 50 pages long. She has already read 22 pages. How many pages are left to read?

   _____ pages

5. Veronica needs 45 points to earn a star. She gets 5 points when she answers a question correctly. If she answers 4 questions correctly, how many more points does she need for a star?

   _____ points

6. Malachi gives out two sheets of paper to each of 30 students. He gives paper to 19 students and has to get more. How many more sheets of paper does he need?

   _____ sheets

Practice Regrouping with 15 to 18

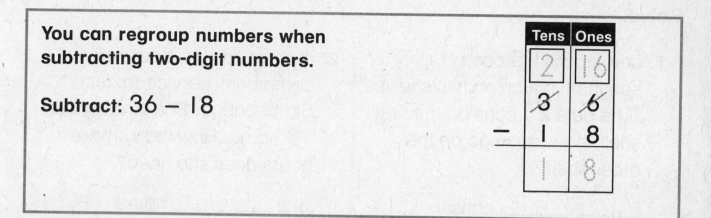

You can regroup numbers when subtracting two-digit numbers.

Subtract: 36 – 18

Subtract. Regroup if you need to.

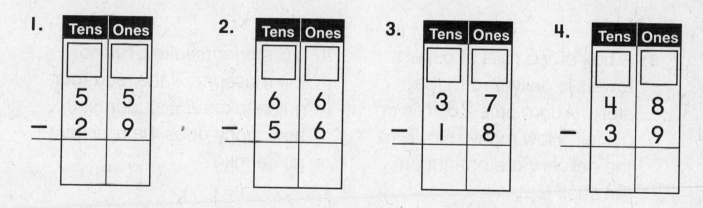

1.
Tens	Ones
5	5
– 2	9

2.
Tens	Ones
6	6
– 5	6

3.
Tens	Ones
3	7
– 1	8

4.
Tens	Ones
4	8
– 3	9

Spiral Review (Chapter 11, Lesson 4) KEY NS 2.2, AF 1.3

Use the table to solve.

5. How many more swimmers than Frisbee players were there?

_____

6. How many more racers than baseball players were there?

_____

Players in the Park	
Activity	**Number**
Swimming	45
Baseball	20
Soccer	16
Frisbee	8
Racing	33

Name _____ Date _____

Practice Regrouping with 15 to 18

Solve.

1. Levi stacks 45 cans of spaghetti sauce on two shelves. If he gets 25 cans on the first shelf, how many go on the other shelf?

   _____ cans

2. Judy needs 36 hours of community service to get a Scout badge. She already has 18 hours. How many more hours does she need?

   _____ hours

3. A box of 96 rolls of paper towels is delivered to the store. Adam puts 28 rolls on a shelf. How many rolls from the delivery are not put on the shelf?

   _____ rolls

4. 46 students take a tour of the museum. If the lead tour guide takes 29 students, how many does the assistant guide take?

   _____ students

5. Arthur collects $22 from Bob and $24 from Michael for a film. He spends $38 on the film. How much of the money did he not spend?

   _____

6. Dotty has 85 tickets for the fair. She uses 24 for the carousel and 24 for the roller coaster. How many tickets does she have left?

   _____ tickets

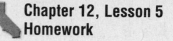
Reasonable Answers

CA Standards
KEY NS 2.2, NS 1.0

Use these steps to solve problems using reason.

Step 1 Read the problem carefully.

Step 2 Ask yourself what you know and what you want to find out.

Step 3 Cross out the answers that are not reasonable.

---

1. John is one grade ahead of his sister Mary. Mary is 9 years old. How old is John?

   8   10   20

2. The cheapest CD player is $12 and the most expensive is $45. Ramone buys one that is in the middle. How much does he spend?

   $10 $25 $50

3. Roger weighs more than Allen, and Allen weighs more than Paul. If Allen weighs 58 lbs, how much does Paul weigh?

   55 lb   60 lb   65 lb

Spiral Review   (Chapter 11, Lesson 4) **KEY** NS 2.2, AF 1.3

Use the table to solve.

4. How many people preferred grapes to berries?

   _____

5. How many people preferred apples and oranges?

   _____

Fruit Preference	
Preferred Fruit	**Number**
Apples	20
Grapes	15
Oranges	16
Bananas	24
Berries	8

Use with text pp. 237–240

Name _____ Date _____

Reasonable Answers

CA Standards
KEY NS 2.2, NS 1.0

Solve.

1. Joe is 10 years old. Jack is 14 years old. Mike is older than Joe but younger than Jack. How old is Mike?

   8   12   16

2. Norma has 40 ribbons. She gives 10 to Elise and some more to Anna. How many ribbons does she have left?

   25   30   35

3. The theater sold 85 tickets. It sold 45 adult tickets and a few senior tickets. How many children's tickets did it sell?

   40   30   50

4. Johnny walks to school. He passes the post office on the way. The post office is half a mile from his house. How far is the school from his house?

   50 ft   200 ft   I mile

5. Apples cost $1 a pound. Oranges cost $2.50 a pound. Grapefruits cost more than oranges. How much do grapefruits cost per pound?

   $1 $2 $3

6. Moise can lift 25 pounds. He is sent to buy 10-pound bags of potatoes. How many bags can he lift at one time?

   1   2   3

Name _____ Date _____

Hands On: Different Ways to Subtract

CA Standards
KEY NS 2.2, MR 1.1

Here are different ways to subtract: mental math, hundred chart, tens and ones blocks, paper and pencil.

$45 - 10 = \underline{35}$

Way that I chose to subtract: mental math

Explanation: can count back 10 from 45 to 35

Choose a way to subtract. Explain how you find the difference.

1. $59 - 31 =$

_____

_____

_____

2. $67 - 6 =$

_____

_____

_____

3. $54 - 17 =$

_____

_____

_____

_____

4. $83 - 46 =$

_____

_____

_____

_____

Spiral Review (Chapter 12, Lesson 1) **KEY** NS 2.2, MR 1.2

5. To subtract 30 from 65 using a hundred chart, what do you do?

_____

6. To subtract 41 from 78 using a hundred chart, what do you do?

_____

Hands On: Different Ways To Subtract

CA Standards
KEY NS 2.2, MR 1.1

Choose a way to solve. Use mental math, a hundred chart, pencil and paper, or tens and ones blocks.

1. "All Wound Up" sells wind-up toys. It has 37 wind-up dancing bears. Wu buys 10 of them to give as favors at his birthday party. How many wind-up dancing bears are left at the store?

   _____

2. A box at the store has 97 wind-up marching feet toys. The store puts 30 of the marching feet toys on display. How many are still in the box?

   _____

3. The store has 67 wind-up clicking teeth. Mr. Washington buys 48 to give as prizes at the fair. How many wind-up clicking teeth are left at the store?

   _____

4. The store has 35 wind-up jumping frogs. Marla buys 12 to give out at her birthday party. How many jumping frogs are left at the store?

   _____

5. The corner grocery wants to buy 125 wind-up drumming bears. The store has 250 wind-up drumming bears. How many more drumming bears does the store have than the grocery wants?

   _____

6. The store has 50 wind-up airplanes. Jenny buys 10 and Joey buys 15. How many wind-up airplanes are left?

   _____

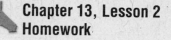
Estimate Differences

CA Standards
NS 6.0, NS 2.0

20 21 22 23 24 25 26 27 28 29 30 31 32 33 34 35 36 37 38 39 40

When you do not need an exact answer, you can estimate.
Round each number to the nearest ten.
Estimate the difference.

$37 - 23 =$ __40__ $-$ __20__ $=$ __20__

Round each number to the nearest ten.
Estimate the difference.

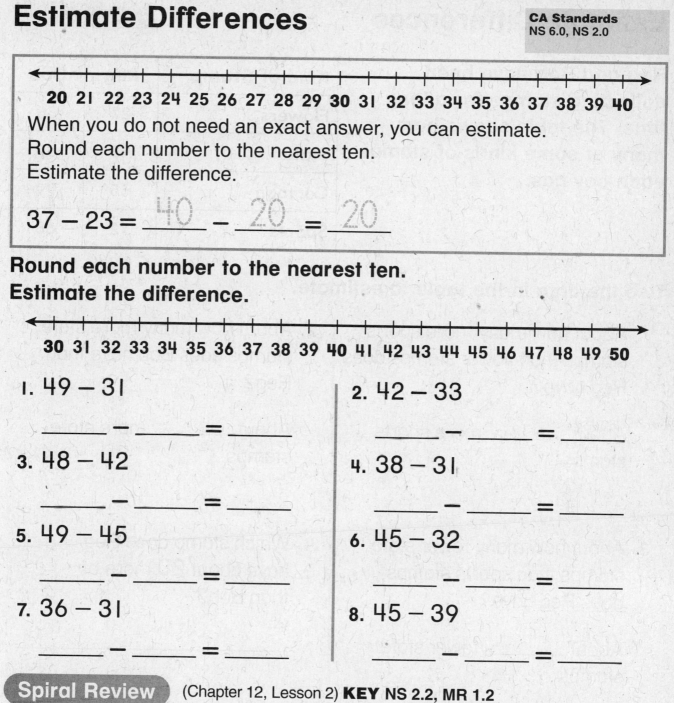

30 31 32 33 34 35 36 37 38 39 40 41 42 43 44 45 46 47 48 49 50

1. $49 - 31$

____ $-$ ____ $=$ ____

2. $42 - 33$

____ $-$ ____ $=$ ____

3. $48 - 42$

____ $-$ ____ $=$ ____

4. $38 - 31$

____ $-$ ____ $=$ ____

5. $49 - 45$

____ $-$ ____ $=$ ____

6. $45 - 32$

____ $-$ ____ $=$ ____

7. $36 - 31$

____ $-$ ____ $=$ ____

8. $45 - 39$

____ $-$ ____ $=$ ____

Spiral Review (Chapter 12, Lesson 2) **KEY** NS 2.2, MR 1.2

9. A rose costs 45¢ and a carnation costs 30¢. How much less does the carnation cost?

_____

10. The Lakers scored 97 points and the Pacers scored 83 points. How many more points did the Lakers score?

_____

Estimate Differences

CA Standards
NS 6.0, NS 2.0

Reg and Bob have been collecting stamps for a long time. The table shows how many of some kinds of stamps each boy has.

Kind of Stamp	Reg	Bob
Flowers	27	38
State	43	57
Cartoon	65	49
Sports	72	68

Use the data in the table to estimate.

1. About how many more sports stamps than flower stamps does Reg have?

   About _____ more sports stamps

2. About how many more state stamps does Bob have than Reg?

   About _____ more state stamps

3. About how many fewer state stamps than sports stamps does Reg have?

   About _____ fewer state stamps

4. Which stamp does Reg have about 20 more of than Bob?

   _____

5. Who has more flower and cartoon stamps, Reg or Bob?

   _____

6. Estimate who has more stamps, Reg or Bob?

   _____

Use with text pp. 249–250

Line Up Digits to Subtract

CA Standards
KEY NS 2.2, NS 2.0

Find 67 − 59.

You can rewrite subtraction problems in vertical form to help you solve them.

Tens	Ones
6	7
− 5	9

Tens	Ones
5	7
6	7
− 5	9
0	8

Write the numbers in vertical form. Subtract.

1. 41 − 19 =

Tens	Ones
−	

2. 55 − 41 =

Tens	Ones
−	

3. 71 − 22 =

Tens	Ones
−	

4. 23 − 8 =

Tens	Ones
−	

5. 78 − 22 =   6. 33 − 16 =   7. 40 − 17 =   8. 88 − 45 =

_____   _____   _____   _____

Spiral Review (Chapter 12, Lesson 3) **KEY NS 2.2, NS 2.0**

9. Mr. Mathews is 42 years old. Mr. Gray is 29 years old. How much older is Mr. Mathews than Mr. Gray?

_____

10. Brenda ran the race last week in 84 seconds. This week she ran it in 67 seconds. How much faster was she this week?

_____

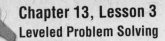
Line Up Digits to Subtract

CA Standards
KEY NS 2.2, NS 2.0

Solve.

1. It usually takes 55 minutes to get from Lakewood to Oakdale. This morning the train is 10 minutes early. How many minutes did the trip take?

   _____

2. Rhonda has 35 minutes to complete a 2-part test. Part 1 took her 15 minutes. How much time does Rhonda have left for part 2?

   _____

3. There are 87 riders on the train. 26 riders get off at the Greenwood station. How many riders are left on the train?

   _____

4. Roberto bikes for 24 minutes more than he runs. If he bikes for 45 minutes, how long does he run?

   _____

5. The biography of Jonas Salk is 15 pages shorter than the biography of Einstein. Einstein's biography is 71 pages long. How long is Salk's biography?

   _____

6. Marvin can carry 10 books. Mimi can carry 8 books. They start to empty a shelf of 35 books. How many are left after they take their first load of books?

   _____

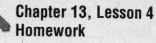
Add and Subtract Money

CA Standards
KEY NS 5.2, **KEY** NS 2.2

You add and subtract money the same way you add and subtract two-digit numbers.

Add or subtract.

$$\begin{array}{r} 5\,14 \\ \cancel{6}\cancel{4}¢ \\ -\,27¢ \\ \hline 37¢ \end{array}$$

$$\begin{array}{r} 40¢ \\ +\,40¢ \\ \hline 80¢ \end{array}$$

Rewrite the numbers. Then add or subtract.

$$84¢ - 9¢ \qquad 26¢ + 12¢$$

$$\begin{array}{r} 7\,14 \\ \cancel{8}\cancel{4}¢ \\ -\,9¢ \\ \hline 75¢ \end{array}$$

$$\begin{array}{r} 26¢ \\ +\,12¢ \\ \hline 38¢ \end{array}$$

Add or subtract.

1. $\begin{array}{r} 50¢ \\ -\,16¢ \\ \hline \end{array}$
2. $\begin{array}{r} 67¢ \\ +\,24¢ \\ \hline \end{array}$
3. $\begin{array}{r} 41¢ \\ -\,5¢ \\ \hline \end{array}$
4. $\begin{array}{r} 35¢ \\ +\,11¢ \\ \hline \end{array}$
5. $\begin{array}{r} 79¢ \\ -\,44¢ \\ \hline \end{array}$

Rewrite the numbers. Then add or subtract.

6. $30¢ - 16¢$ 7. $78¢ + 11¢$ 8. $98¢ - 79¢$ 9. $39¢ + 5¢$

$-$ $+$ $-$ $+$

Spiral Review (Chapter 12, Lesson 4) **KEY NS 2.2, NS 2.0**

10. Martha has to read 48 pages by Monday. She read 19 pages on Saturday. How many pages are left to read?

_____

11. The deli has a barrel with 47 pickles. The team goes and buys 29 pickles. How many are left in the barrel?

_____

Name _____ Date _____

Add and Subtract Money

CA Standards
KEY NS 5.2, KEY NS 2.2

Solve.

1. Melanie has 40 pennies. She shares 10 pennies with Melissa. How many pennies does Melanie have left?

_____

2. Katie has 30¢ in her purse. She finds a dime on the street and she puts that in her purse. How much money is in her purse?

_____

3. Jeff put 75¢ into his bank on Monday. Then he put 20¢ in the bank on Tuesday. How much money did he put in those two days?

_____

4. Manuel had a $50 bill. He bought a pair of pants for $24 with it. How much change did he get back?

_____

5. Craig wants to buy an apple for 55¢. He pays with 2 quarters and a dime. How much change does he get back?

_____

6. 5 of Lanie's friends each gave her $2 to buy a book, and Lanie added her own $2. The book cost $11. How much change did she get back?

_____

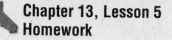
Check Subtraction

CA Standards
KEY NS 2.1, MR 2.2

After you find the difference, you can add to check your subtraction.

$$\begin{array}{r} 47 \\ -28 \\ \hline 19 \end{array} \qquad \begin{array}{r} \boxed{19} \\ +\boxed{28} \\ \hline \boxed{47} \end{array}$$

Subtract. Check by adding.

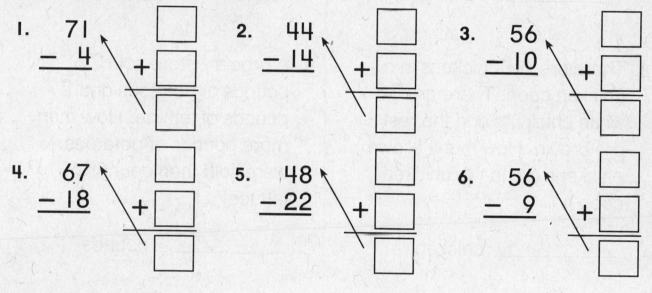

1. $\begin{array}{r} 71 \\ -\ 4 \\ \hline \end{array}$ $\boxed{}$ $+\boxed{}$ $\boxed{}$

2. $\begin{array}{r} 44 \\ -14 \\ \hline \end{array}$ $\boxed{}$ $+\boxed{}$ $\boxed{}$

3. $\begin{array}{r} 56 \\ -10 \\ \hline \end{array}$ $\boxed{}$ $+\boxed{}$ $\boxed{}$

4. $\begin{array}{r} 67 \\ -18 \\ \hline \end{array}$ $\boxed{}$ $+\boxed{}$ $\boxed{}$

5. $\begin{array}{r} 48 \\ -22 \\ \hline \end{array}$ $\boxed{}$ $+\boxed{}$ $\boxed{}$

6. $\begin{array}{r} 56 \\ -\ 9 \\ \hline \end{array}$ $\boxed{}$ $+\boxed{}$ $\boxed{}$

Spiral Review (Chapter 12, Lesson 5) **KEY NS 2.2, NS 1.0**

7. Monica is 14 years old. Lucille is 16 years old. Louisa is older than Monica but younger than Lucille. How old is Louisa?

    12   15   18

8. The butcher has 30 chickens. He sells 18 to a restaurant. He gives a few to Mrs. Rose. How many chickens does the butcher have left?

    10   12   15

Use with text pp. 255–256

Check Subtraction

CA Standards
KEY NS 2.1, MR 2.2

Solve and then check your answer.

1. The farmer has 50 bales of hay. He puts 30 on the truck and leaves the rest in the barn. How many bales are in the barn?

_____ bales of hay

2. Jed milks the cows on Mondays. Last Monday, he collected 45 gallons of milk. This week he collected 5 gallons of milk. How many gallons more did he get this week?

_____ gallons

3. There are 64 chickens in a chicken coop. There are 38 white chickens and the rest are brown. How many brown chickens are in the chicken coop?

_____ chicken

4. A grocery store sold 75 pounds of potatoes and 27 pounds of lettuce. How many more pounds of potatoes were sold than pounds of lettuce?

_____ pounds

5. Daphne found 24 red pails and 15 blue pails in her basement. She took 10 pails to the beach, and 5 of them were red. How many blue pails were left at home?

_____

6. Alphonso bought 15 comics. He traded 5 of his to Ali for 8 different comics. He then lent 10 comics to Rina. How many comics did he have left?

_____

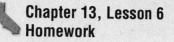
Create and Solve

Growth Chart

Child	Height in September	Height in June
Mansour	51"	54"
Ricardo	49"	53"
Lily	48"	49"
Jessica	50"	55"

1. Who was the tallest in September? _____

2. Who was the tallest in June? _____

3. Who grew the least from September to June? _____

4. Who grew more, the boys or the girls? _____

5. Write your own problem using the Growth Chart.

_____

Spiral Review   (Chapter 12, Lesson 5) **KEY** NS 2.2, NS 1.0

6. Jean is 7. Her sister is Carol is older, but not as old as Rose, who is
   12. How old is Carol?

   6   10   14

7. It is hotter in San Diego than in Palo Alto, but not as hot as in San
   Antonio. Today San Diego reached 89°F. What is the temperature in
   San Antonio?

   75°F   86°F   95°F

Create and Solve

CA Standards
KEY NS 2.2, AF 1.3

Table 1

City	High in °F
New York	103
San Francisco	88
Chicago	92
Houston	115

Table 2

Range in lb	Number
Under 50–54	4
55–59	7
60–64	6
65 and higher	2

1. Write a simple comparison problem about the temperatures in Table 1.

_____

_____

_____

2. Write a simple comparison problem about the weights in Table 2.

_____

_____

_____

3. Write a subtraction problem about temperatures.

_____

_____

4. Write an addition problem about weights.

_____

_____

5. Write a subtraction problem about pairs of temperatures.

_____

_____

_____

6. Write an addition problem about Table 2 as a whole.

_____

_____

_____

Hands On: Sort Shapes

CA Standard
KEY MG 2.1

Geometric shapes may have sides and vertices.

1. Which has more sides, a shape with 6 vertices or a shape with 7 vertices?

_____

2. Which has more vertices, a shape with 4 sides or a shape with 3 sides?

_____

3. Take a shape with 4 sides. Draw a line between two vertices that do not share a side. How many shapes does that make? How many sides do they have?

_____

4. Take a shape with 5 sides. Choose a vertex. Draw lines from that vertex to the other vertices that do not share sides with the first vertex. How many shapes are formed? How many sides do they have?

_____

5. Suppose I have a shape with 10 sides (don't try to draw it). I choose a vertex then draw lines to the other vertices that don't share sides with the first vertex. How many vertices will that be and why?

_____

Spiral Review (Chapter 13, Lesson 1) **KEY** NS 2.2, MR 1.1

6. How would you solve the following: $47 - 28 = ?$

_____

7. Would you use tens and ones blocks to solve $56 - 45 = ?$

_____

Use with text pp. 271–272

Name _____ Date _____

Hands On: Sort Shapes

CA Standard
KEY MG 2.1

Solve.

1. Fred drives around the block looking for a place to park his car. How many sides are in the path he took?

   _____

2. Meredith held a stick from her waist to the sand, and then she turned completely around, making the stick turn with her. How many vertices were in the figure she drew on the sand?

   _____

3. Lisa rode her bike along a path with 4 sides, and Mona rode along a path with 5 sides. Who made more turns, and how many turns did she make?

   _____

4. Can all 4-sided figures be made from 2 triangles? Why?

   _____
   _____
   _____
   _____

5. Can all 5-sided figures be made from 3 triangles? Why?

   _____
   _____
   _____
   _____

6. Can you draw more different kinds of 3-sided shapes or 4-sided shapes?

   _____
   _____
   _____
   _____

Plane Shapes

CA Standard
KEY MG 2.1

A shape with 4 sides is a **quadrilateral.**	A **parallelogram** has opposite sides that are the same distance apart.
A **rhombus** is a parallelogram with 4 sides the same length.	A **trapezoid** has only one pair of opposite sides that are the same distance apart.

1. Draw a circle around every quadrilateral.

2. Draw a circle around every trapezoid.

3. Draw a circle around every rhombus.

4. Draw a circle around every parallelogram.

Spiral Review   (Chapter 13, Lesson 2) NS 6.0, NS 2.0

5. Estimate the difference between 53 and 37. _____

6. Estimate the difference between 38 and 12. _____

Use with text pp. 273–274

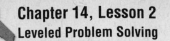
Plane Shapes

CA Standard
KEY MG 2.1

Name the shape.

1. It has 3 sides and 3 vertices.

_____

2. It has no sides and no vertices.

_____

3. It has 4 sides. All of its sides are equal. All of its angles are right angles.

_____

4. It does not have 4 sides. All of its sides are equal. All of its angles are acute.

_____

5. It has 4 sides. All of its angles are right angles. Its 4 sides are not all the same length.

_____

6. It can be formed by cutting a triangle off each of the four corners of a rectangle.

_____

Name _____ Date _____

Compare Plane Shapes

CA Standard
KEY MG 2.1

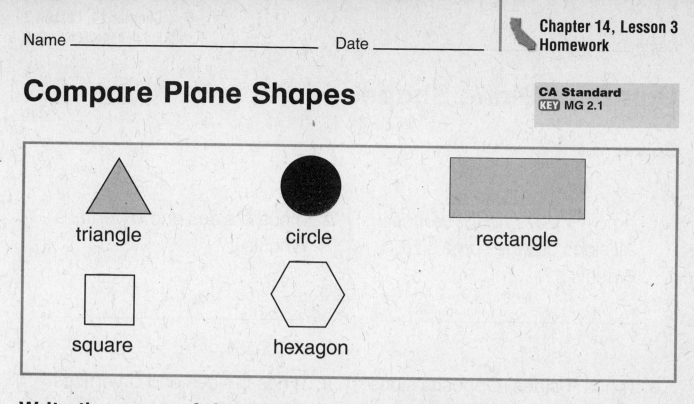

triangle   circle   rectangle

square   hexagon

Write the name of the shape. Write two reasons for your answer.

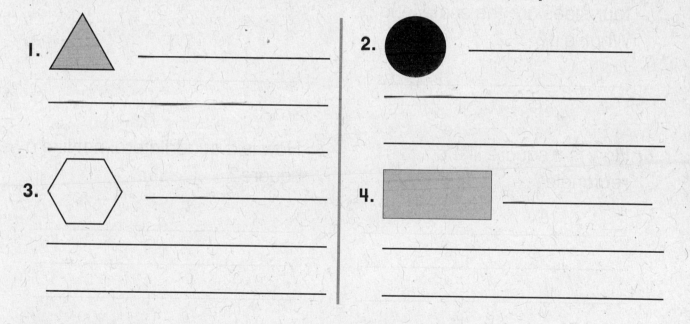

1. _____

_____

_____

2. _____

_____

_____

3. _____

_____

_____

4. _____

_____

_____

Spiral Review   (Chapter 13, Lesson 3) **KEY NS 2.2, NS 2.0**

5. You want to solve $54 - 21 = ?$ Which answer is correct: 33 or 42?

_____

6. You want to solve $93 - 28 = ?$ Which answer is correct: 65 or 11?

_____

Compare Plane Shapes

CA Standard
KEY MG 2.1

Solve.

1. It has 4 sides and 4 vertices. All sides are the same size. What is it?

_____

2. It has 6 sides and 6 vertices. What is it?

_____

3. It has 4 sides. Opposite sides are the same length, but not all four sides are the same length. What is it?

_____

4. It has 5 sides and 5 vertices. What is it?

_____

5. How is a square like a rectangle?

_____

_____

_____

_____

6. How is a quadrilateral not like a square?

_____

_____

_____

_____

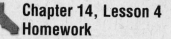
Hands On: Combine and Separate Shapes

CA Standards
KEY MG 2.2, MR 1.2

You can cut shapes apart to make other shapes.
Use blocks to make this shape. Draw the blocks.

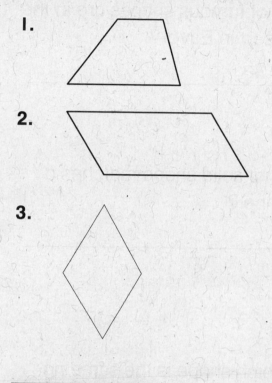

1.

2.

3.

Spiral Review (Chapter 13, Lesson 4) **KEY** NS 5.2, **KEY** NS 2.2

4. Carl owes Rita 34¢ and Nina owes her 47¢. How much money do they owe Rita?

_____

5. John has 80¢ and buys a ball for 57¢. How much money does he have left?

_____

Use with text pp. 279–280

Name _____ Date _____

Hands On: Combine and Separate Shapes

CA Standard
KEY MG 2.2, MR 1.2

Solve.

1. What solid shape matches a box of cereal?

   _____

2. What famous shapes are in the desert in Egypt?

   _____

3. What solid shape matches a can of tuna?

   _____

4. What solid shape matches a funnel?

   _____

5. Which shape is easier to balance on a stick, a cube or a sphere? Why?

   _____

   _____

   _____

   _____

6. Which shape is the same no matter how you look at it, from any angle or direction?

   _____

Make New Shapes

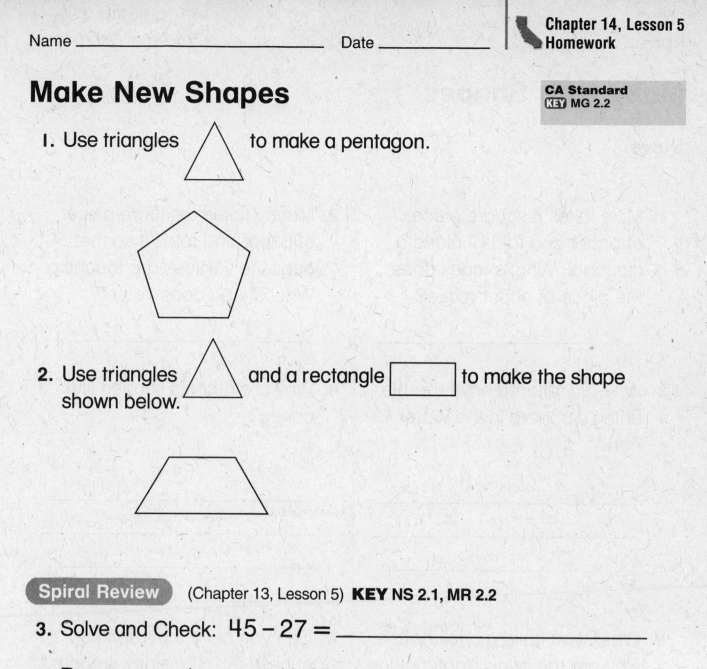

1. Use triangles △ to make a pentagon.

2. Use triangles △ and a rectangle ☐ to make the shape shown below.

Spiral Review (Chapter 13, Lesson 5) **KEY NS 2.1, MR 2.2**

3. Solve and Check: $45 - 27 =$ _____

4. Rosa goes to the store with 85¢ and spends 60¢. The clerk gives her a quarter change. How does Rosa check if the change is correct?

_____

Name _____ Date _____

Make New Shapes

CA Standard
KEY MG 2.2

Solve.

1. Mike takes a square piece of paper and folds it along a diagonal. What shapes does the piece of paper make?

   _____

2. Manny takes a square piece of paper and folds it so that opposite vertices are touching. What shape does he get?

   _____

3. Why did Mildred have trouble riding a sphere in the Water Park?

   _____

   _____

   _____

4. Why are funnels shaped like cones?

   _____

   _____

   _____

5. When you build a brick house, why are the bricks rectangular prisms and not cubes?

   _____

   _____

   _____

   _____

6. Can you build a pyramid out of cubes? Are the sides smooth?

   _____

   _____

   _____

   _____

Hands On: Solid Shapes

Write the names of the two solid shapes in each picture.

1. _____

   _____

2. _____

3. _____

4. _____

Spiral Review (Chapter 14, Lesson 1) KEY MG 2.1

Circle the shapes that match the description.

5. 0 sides, 0 vertices

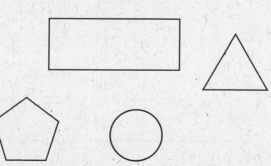

6. 3 sides, 3 vertices

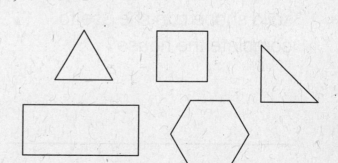

145

Use with text pp. 291–292

Hands On: Solid Shapes

CA Standards
KEY MG 2.0, MR 2.0, MR 1.2

Solve.

1. David collected 4 objects:

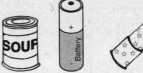

Which solid shape matches the objects in David's collection?

_____

2. Maria buys 12 △ for her birthday party. Which solid shape matches the shape of the hats?

_____

3. Toshiro used solid shapes to build the train below. Which solid figures did he use in building the train?

_____

4. Mrs. Jackson buys a box of pasta, a box of cereal and a can of orange juice. Which two solid shapes match the objects she buys?

_____

5. Carmen builds a house with solid shapes. If she uses a pyramid for the roof, which solid shape can she use to complete the house?

_____

6. What solid shape do you need to combine with the shape below to make a table?

_____

146
Use with text pp. 291–292

Hands On: Faces, Edges, and Vertices

CA Standard
KEY MG 2.1

Circle the shapes that match the description.

1. 1 face, 0 edges, 0 vertices

 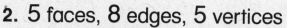 

2. 5 faces, 8 edges, 5 vertices

3. 6 faces, 12 edges, 8 vertices

  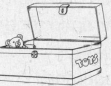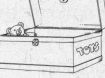

4. 2 faces, 0 edges, 0 vertices

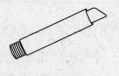  

Spiral Review (Chapter 14, Lesson 2) **KEY** MG 2.1

Circle the shapes that match each name.

5. pentagon

6. triangle

7. rectangle

Hands On: Faces, Edges, and Vertices

CA Standard
KEY MG 2.1

Solve.

1. I am a solid figure with 5 faces, 8 edges, and 5 vertices. Which of the figures shown below am I?

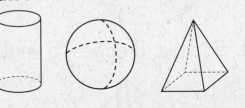

_____

2. Serena draws a figure that slides, stacks, and rolls. Which of the figures below did Serena draw?

_____

3. Ingrid wants to paint the faces of a rectangular prism, a pyramid, and a cylinder. How many faces she will paint altogether?

_____

4. Two solid shapes have the same number of faces, vertices and edges. Write the name of the two shapes.

_____

5. Devon combines 2 solid shapes. Together the shapes have 8 faces, 12 edges, and 8 vertices. One of the shapes is a rectangular prism. What is the second shape?

6. Maya, Jack, and Chen each have a solid shape. Maya's shape has more than 5 faces. Jack's shape has 4 fewer faces than Maya's. Chen's shape has the same number of edges and vertices as Jack's. Write the name of the shape each child has.

_____

_____

_____

Hands On: Identify Faces

CA Standard
KEY MG 2.1

Draw the shapes you would make if you traced the faces of the object. Use models to help.

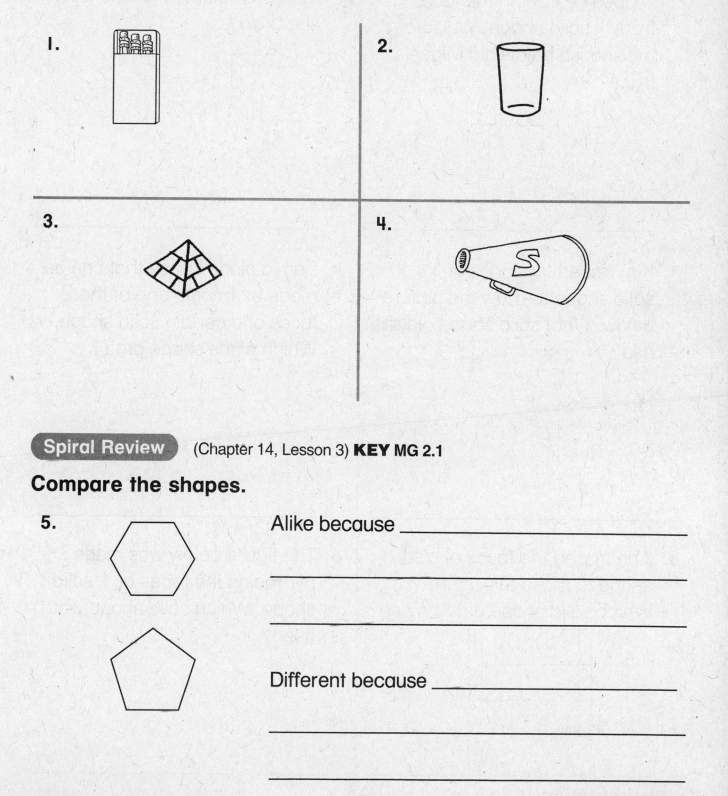

1.

2.

3.

4.

Spiral Review (Chapter 14, Lesson 3) **KEY** MG 2.1

Compare the shapes.

5.

Alike because _____

_____

_____

Different because _____

_____

Name _____ Date _____

Hands On: Identify Faces

CA Standard
KEY MG 2.1

1. Miguel draws 2 different plane shapes by tracing the faces from 1 solid shape. Which of the shapes below did Miguel trace?

2. Maya traced a face of the solid below. What plane shape does she draw?

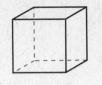

_____

3. Kim traced the faces of 1 solid shape to draw the picture below. What solid shape did she use?

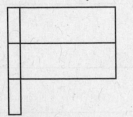

4. I am a plane shape that can be made by tracing one of the 2 faces of a certain solid shape. Which plane shape am I?

_____

5. Ann traced the faces of a solid shape to make this figure. Which solid shape did Ann use?

6. The figure below was made by tracing the faces of 1 solid shape. Which solid shape was used?

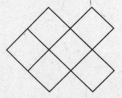

_____

Use with text pp. 295–296

Compare Plane and Solid Shapes

CA Standard
KEY MG 2.1

Write how the shapes are alike and different.
Count the faces, edges, and vertices.

	Alike	Different
1. 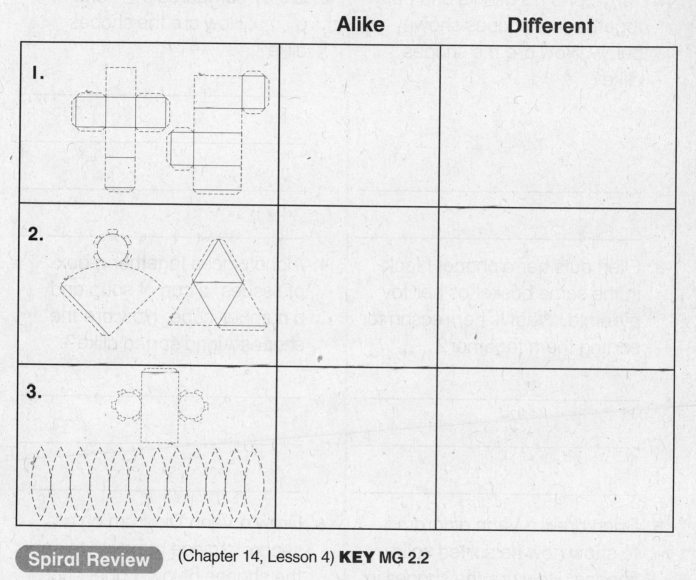		
2.		
3.		

Spiral Review (Chapter 14, Lesson 4) **KEY** MG 2.2

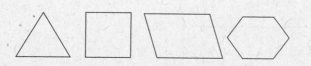

4. Alex made the shape above using 2 pattern blocks. Circle the pattern blocks she used.

Name _____ Date _____

Compare Plane and Solid Shapes

Solve.

1. Tony sorts his blocks and puts together the shapes shown below. How are the shapes alike?

   _____

   _____

2. Sandy compares a ⬜ and a ⬛. How are the shapes alike?

   _____

   _____

   _____

3. Ellen puts her alphabet block in the same basket as her toy pyramid. What is her reason for sorting them together?

   _____

   _____

4. Alana places together a box of tissues, a can of soup and a number cube. How are the shapes Alana sorted alike?

   _____

   _____

5. Brian drew a Venn diagram to show how he sorted solid shapes. How are the shapes in the overlapping part of the Venn diagram alike?

   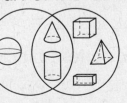

   _____

   _____

6. Draw a Venn Diagram on a separate piece of paper to sort the shapes below. Label each section to show how the shapes are alike.

   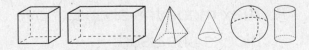

Geometric Patterns

CA Standards
KEY SDAP 2.0, SDAP 2.1

Find the pattern.

1. Janey is making a pattern for her mom. Draw the shape that is likely to come next in the pattern?

2. Ryan is putting beads on a bracelet. This is the pattern he makes.

   What is missing? _____

3. Sarah sees this pattern in a scarf at the store.

   Is the pattern growing or repeating? _____

   Draw the pattern units.

Spiral Review (Chapter 14, Lesson 5) **KEY** MG 2.2

4. Jordan traced 2 pattern blocks to make this shape. Draw a line to show which pattern blocks Jordan used.

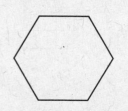

5. Ann used 2 pattern blocks to make this shape. Draw a line to show how she placed the blocks. Then draw the pattern blocks showing a different shape.

Geometric Patterns

CA Standards
KEY SDAP 2.0, SDAP 2.1

Solve.

1. I am a solid figure with 6 faces, 12 edges, and 8 vertices. Which of the figures shown below am I?

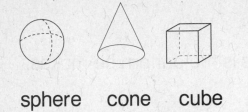

sphere   cone   cube

2. Look at the shapes below. Draw the pattern unit.

3. Leo made a beaded bracelet showing the pattern below. Draw the shape that comes next in the pattern.

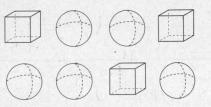

4. John traced the faces of solid shapes to design a border for his bedroom. Which solid shape will he most likely trace next to continue the pattern?

_____

_____

5. Mr. Yi drew the pattern below on the board. Draw the same type of pattern using solid shapes. Then show which solid shape would most likely come next.

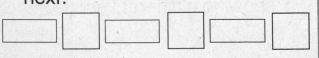

6. Natalia designs a pattern for art class. Draw the shape that will come next.

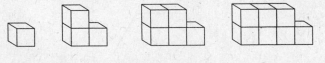

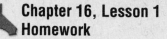
Hands On: Halves and Fourths

Fractions divide a whole into parts. Together all the parts make a whole.

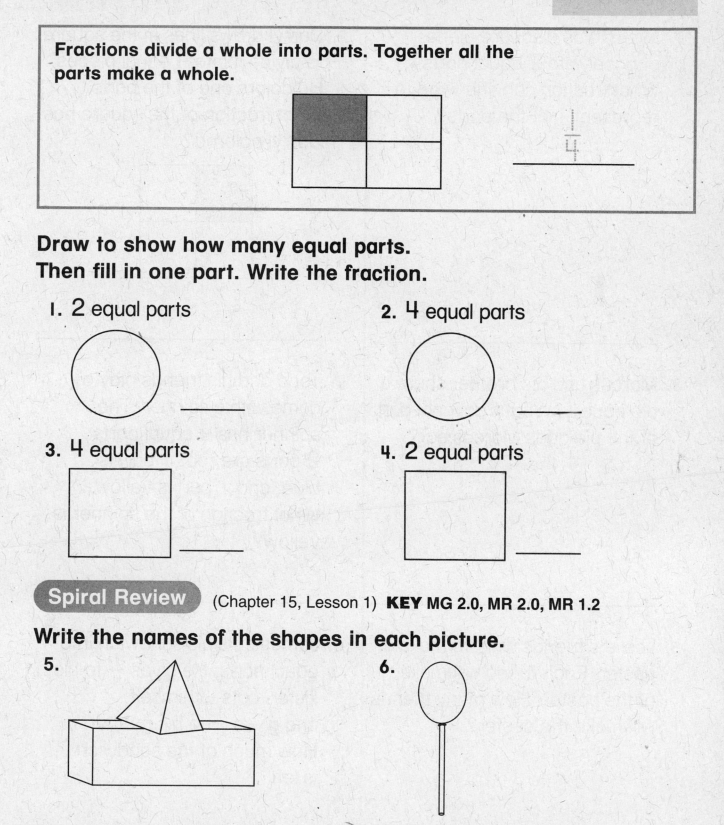

Draw to show how many equal parts.
Then fill in one part. Write the fraction.

1. 2 equal parts

_____

2. 4 equal parts

_____

3. 4 equal parts

_____

4. 2 equal parts

_____

Spiral Review (Chapter 15, Lesson 1) **KEY** MG 2.0, MR 2.0, MR 1.2

Write the names of the shapes in each picture.

5.

6.

_____   _____

Use with text pp. 309–310

Hands On: Halves and Fourths

CA Standards
KEY NS 4.1, KEY NS 4.2

1. Maya folds a square piece of paper into 2 equal parts. What fraction can she write to represent 1 of the parts?

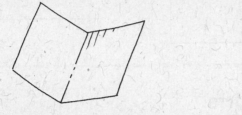

_____

2. Darryl draws lines in the square to divide it into 4 equal pieces. He colors one of the parts. What fraction of the square has Darryl colored?

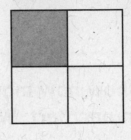

_____

3. Marcus and his brother share a pie equally. What fractional part of the pie does Marcus eat?

_____

4. Todd and his friends play a game with a spinner. The spinner has 4 equal parts. 2 parts are red, 1 part is blue, and 1 part is yellow. What fraction of the spinner is yellow?

_____

5. Leslie's friends want to make a poster. Each friend will make $\frac{1}{4}$ of the poster. How many friends will make the poster?

_____

6. James cuts his sandwich into equal parts. He gives $\frac{1}{4}$ to his sister, eats $\frac{1}{4}$ himself, and gives $\frac{1}{4}$ to his mother. How much of the sandwich is left?

_____

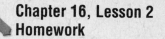
Unit Fractions

CA Standards
KEY NS 4.1, **KEY** NS 4.2

> Fractions name equal parts of a whole.
>
> A unit fraction names one of the equal parts.
>
> The fraction $\frac{1}{2}$ means 1 part of 2 equal parts.
>
>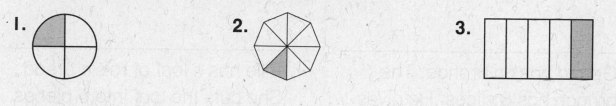

Write the fraction for the shaded part.

1. ⊕ _____

2. ⬡ _____

3. ▭ _____

4. Rory cuts a pie into 4 equal pieces. What fraction
names one part of the whole? Circle the fraction.

$\frac{1}{2}$ $\frac{1}{3}$ $\frac{1}{4}$ $\frac{1}{5}$

Spiral Review (Chapter 15, Lesson 2) **KEY** MG 2.1

Circle the shapes that match the description.

5. 0 faces, 0 edges, 0 vertices

6. 6 faces, 12 edges, 8 vertices

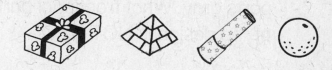

Name _____ Date _____

Unit Fractions

1. Flora draws a shape on the board. She draws lines to divide the shape into 3 equal pieces. Then she colors 1 part of the shape. What fraction of the shape does Flora color?

2. Luis displays a banner for the pep rally. The banner is made up of 8 equal parts. He places stars in one of the 8 sections. What fraction of the banner has stars?

_____

3. Gerald has an orange. The orange has 8 slices. He gives one slice to Suzie. What fraction names how many pieces he gives to Suzie?

4. Ellie has a loaf of raisin bread. She cuts the loaf into 6 pieces. She gives 1 piece to her friend. What fraction names how much of the bread she gave to her friend?

_____

5. Leon draws a design for art class. The design is divided into 12 parts. Leon shades 11 of the parts gray. What fractional part of the design is NOT gray?

6. Ella and 6 friends make a quilt. They each make an equal part of the quilt. What fractional part of the quilt does each child make?

_____

More About Fractions

CA Standards
KEY NS 4.2, NS 4.0

> **Fractions can name more than one equal part of a whole.**
>
> There are 4 equal parts.
>
> 3 parts are shaded.
>
> 3 fourths are shaded.
>
> $\frac{3}{4}$ are shaded.

Write the fraction for the shaded parts.

1. $\frac{4}{5}$

2. _____

3. _____

4. Fold a sheet of paper in half. Fold it in half again.
   Fold the paper diagonally. Open the paper. Color 2 parts.
   What fraction did you color?

   _____

Spiral Review (Chapter 15, Lesson 3) **KEY** MG 2.1

Draw the shapes you would make if you traced the faces of the object.

5.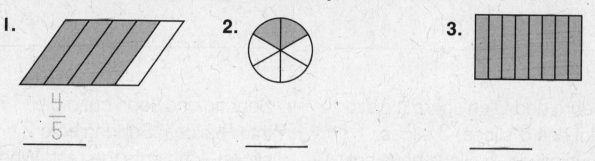

6.

Name _____ Date _____

More About Fractions

1. Maria's friends play a game with this spinner. The spinner has 5 equal parts. Two parts are gray, and the rest is white. What fractional part of the spinner is gray?

_____

2. The board for a game has 9 squares. Three of them are black. The rest are white. What fraction of the board is black?

_____

3. Debra and Glen share a pizza that has 8 slices. 3 slices have olives. 5 slices have hot peppers. What fraction names the part of the pizza that has olives?

_____

4. Sabrina and John cut a pie into 4 slices. Sabrina eats 2 slices. John eats the rest. What fraction names the part of the pie that John eats?

_____

5. Jordan drew 15 circles. He colored 3 circles green and 7 yellow. What fractional part of the set is left to color?

_____

6. Indira gets 12 birthday presents. She opens $\frac{2}{3}$ of them. How many presents does she have left to open?

_____

Wholes and Parts

CA Standards
KEY NS 4.3, KEY NS 4.2

A fraction can name one whole or more than one whole.

$\frac{6}{6} = 1$

$\frac{6}{6}$ are gray.

Six sixths are gray.

8 parts are shaded

$\frac{8}{6}$ are shaded.

Eight sixths are shaded.

Circle the fraction that names the shaded part.

1.

$\frac{8}{8}$ $\frac{12}{8}$ $\frac{12}{16}$

2.

$\frac{9}{5}$ $\frac{9}{10}$ $\frac{10}{10}$

3.

$\frac{1}{8}$ $\frac{1}{1}$ $\frac{8}{8}$

4. Simon ate $\frac{3}{2}$ slices of an apple. Did he eat less than a whole apple, the whole apple, or more than the whole apple. Draw a picture to show your answer.

_____

Spiral Review (Chapter 15, Lesson 4) **KEY** MG 2.1

Describe how the shapes are alike and how they are different.

_____

_____

_____

Use with text pp. 317–318

Wholes and Parts

CA Standard
KEY NS 4.3, **KEY** NS 4.2

1. Toshiro has 2 apples that are each cut into 4 equal parts. He eats 6 parts. How many fourths does he eat?

_____

2. Lisette drew a rectangle and divided it into fourths. She colored the whole rectangle. How many fourths were colored?

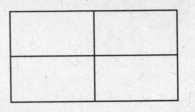

_____

3. Mrs. Jackson's class is having a pizza party. There are 2 pizzas each cut into 8 slices. The class ate 8 slices from the first pizza and 3 slices form the second. What fractional part of a pizza was eaten?

_____

4. Valarie makes 2 pans of brownies for a bake sale. She cuts each pan into 12 brownies. She sells 15 brownies. What fractional part of a pan of brownies did Valarie sell?

_____

5. A baker bakes 4 loaves of bread for a party. Each loaf of bread is sliced into 10 pieces. 18 people eat 2 slices of bread. What is the fraction that shows how many loaves of bread were eaten?

_____

6. Draw and write the fraction of the bread that was not eaten in problem 5.

_____

Use a Picture

CA Standards
KEY NS 4.2, MR 1.2

You can use a picture to find a fraction.
You can use a picture to compare two fractions.

Use the pictures to solve each problem. Color to solve the problem.

1. Azim brings 10 balloons to a party. 5 of them are red. What fraction of the balloons are red?

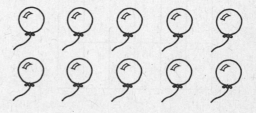

_____ balloons

2. Sammi cuts a pizza into 8 equal parts. She eats 2 pieces. What fraction of the pizza is left?

_____ pizza

3. Sharon plants 5 rows of vegetables in the garden. 2 rows are of yellow vegetables. 3 rows are of green vegetables. What fraction of the garden has green vegetables?

_____

Spiral Review (Chapter 15, Lesson 5) **KEY** SDAP 2.0, SDAP 2.1

4. Patty makes a design for the border of her treasure box. Draw the shape that is most likely to come next in the design.

Use a Picture

CA Standard
KEY NS 4.1, MR 1.2,

1. Cassie cuts a cake into 12 equal pieces. Her friends eat 8 pieces of the cake. What fraction of the cake do they eat?

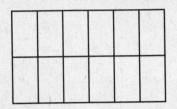

_____

2. Darla cuts an apple into 6 equal pieces. She eats 5 pieces. What fractional part of the apple did she eat?

_____

3. Ellen eats 4 pieces of a cake that was cut into 8 equal pieces. What fraction of the cake was not eaten by Ellen?

_____

4. Darren eats $\frac{4}{10}$ of the cherries. Robert eats $\frac{5}{10}$ of the cherries. Was the amount of cherries eaten closer to all of the cherries, half of the cherries, or none of the cherries?

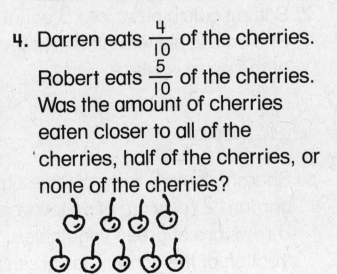

_____

5. Lisa makes a bracelet with 12 beads. 3 beads are red, 3 beads are white, and 3 beads are blue. The remaining beads are clear. What fractional part of the bracelet is made from clear beads?

_____

6. Kim uses 15 shells to make a picture frame. $\frac{2}{3}$ of the shells she uses are white. The remainder are yellow. How many shells used are yellow?

_____

Hands On: Compare Fractions

CA Standards
KEY NS 4.1, MR 1.2

Use the symbols > to show greater
than and < to show less than
to compare fractions.

$\frac{1}{3}$ (>) $\frac{1}{6}$

1. $\frac{1}{2}$ ◯ $\frac{1}{4}$

2. $\frac{1}{8}$ ◯ $\frac{1}{4}$

3. $\frac{1}{4}$ ◯ $\frac{1}{8}$

4. $\frac{6}{12}$ ◯ $\frac{1}{2}$

5. You ate $\frac{1}{3}$ of a pizza. Your friend ate $\frac{1}{4}$ of the same pizza.
Who ate more of the pizza?

Spiral Review (Chapter 16, Lesson 1) **KEY** NS 4.1, **KEY** NS 4.2

Draw to show how many equal parts. Then fill in one part. Write the fraction.

6. 2 equal parts

_____

7. 4 equal parts

_____

Use with text pp. 327–328

Hands On: Compare Fractions

CA Standards
KEY NS 4.1, MR 1.2

1. Larry cuts his cookie into 3 equal pieces and eats one piece. Maya cuts a cookie of the same size into two equal pieces and eats one piece. Who ate the larger piece of cookie ?

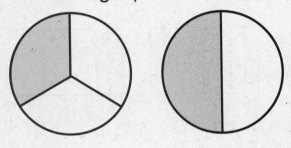

_____

2. Sara cuts a gray sheet of paper into 4 equal parts. She then cuts a white sheet of the same size into 8 equal parts. Which color paper has the larger pieces?

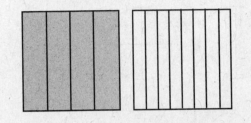

_____

3. Dwayne eats $\frac{1}{9}$ of the raisin bread. Francisco eats $\frac{1}{3}$ of the raisin bread. Who eats more raisin bread?

_____

4. Makoto and Otis each decorate diamond patterns that are the same size and shape. Makoto decorates $\frac{1}{8}$ of a diamond. Otis decorates $\frac{1}{4}$ of a diamond. Who decorates more?

_____

5. Lyle eats $\frac{1}{2}$ of a personal pizza. Carlos eats $\frac{2}{6}$ of a personal pizza. Write a comparison to show who ate the most pizza.

_____
_____
_____

6. Natalia uses $\frac{2}{4}$ of a roll of ribbon to decorate her gift box. Robin uses $\frac{5}{10}$ of a roll of ribbon to decorate her box. Write a comparison to show who used the most of their ribbon.

_____
_____
_____

Use with text pp. 327–328

Hands On: Fractions of a Group

CA Standards
KEY NS 4.2, NS 4.0

Fractions can name parts of a set.

There are 3 hearts in the set.

$\frac{2}{3}$ of the hearts are shaded.

$\frac{1}{3}$ of the hearts is not shaded.

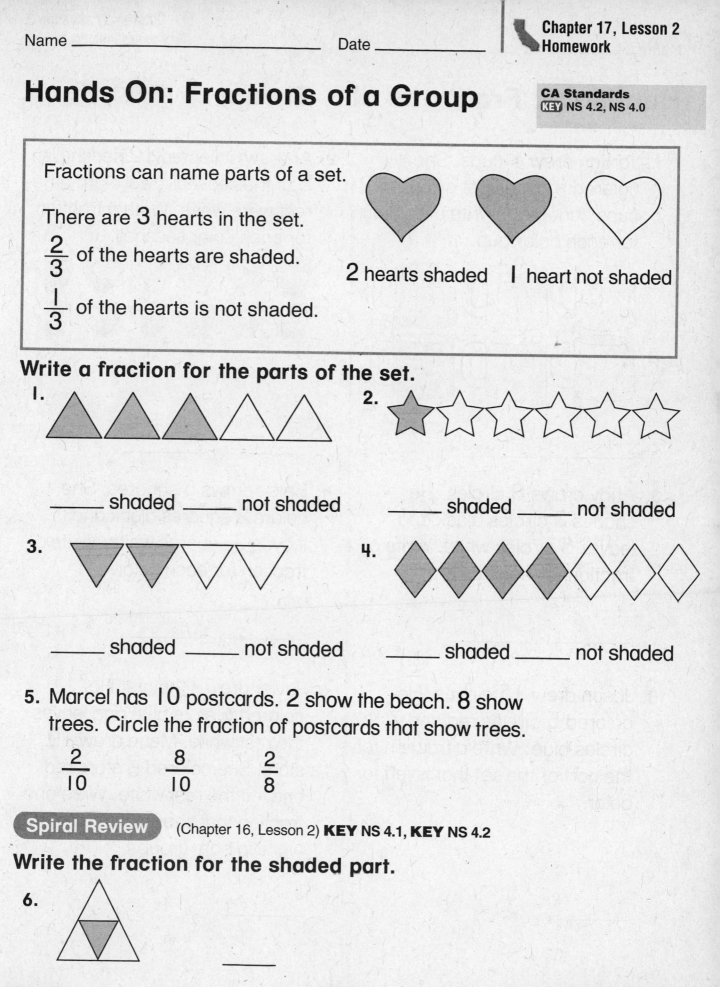

2 hearts shaded   1 heart not shaded

Write a fraction for the parts of the set.

1.

_____ shaded _____ not shaded

2.

_____ shaded _____ not shaded

3.

_____ shaded _____ not shaded

4.

_____ shaded _____ not shaded

5. Marcel has 10 postcards. 2 show the beach. 8 show trees. Circle the fraction of postcards that show trees.

$\frac{2}{10}$ $\frac{8}{10}$ $\frac{2}{8}$

Spiral Review   (Chapter 16, Lesson 2) **KEY** NS 4.1, **KEY** NS 4.2

Write the fraction for the shaded part.

6.

_____

Name _____   Date _____

Hands On: Fractions of a Group

1. Jordan drew 6 cups. She colored 4 cups light gray and 2 cups dark gray. Write a fraction for each color cup.

_____, _____

2. Andrew collected 12 seashells. 5 of the seashells were gray the rest were white. Write a fraction for each color seashell.

_____, _____

3. Andy draws 8 circles. He shades 3 circles black and leaves 5 circles white. Write a fraction for each color.

_____, _____

4. Betsy draws 5 squares. She colors 2 squares black and leaves 3 squares white. Write a fraction for each color.

_____, _____

5. Jason drew 15 circles. He colored 5 circles red and 7 circles blue. Write a fraction for the part of the set that is left to color.

_____

6. Javier drew 12 stars. He colored 6 stars blue and leaves the rest white. Mena drew 10 stars. She colored 5 stars red and left the rest white. Write one fraction that shows the stars left white in both groups.

_____

Fractional Parts of a Group

CA Standard
KEY NS 4.2

You can show a fractional part of a group.

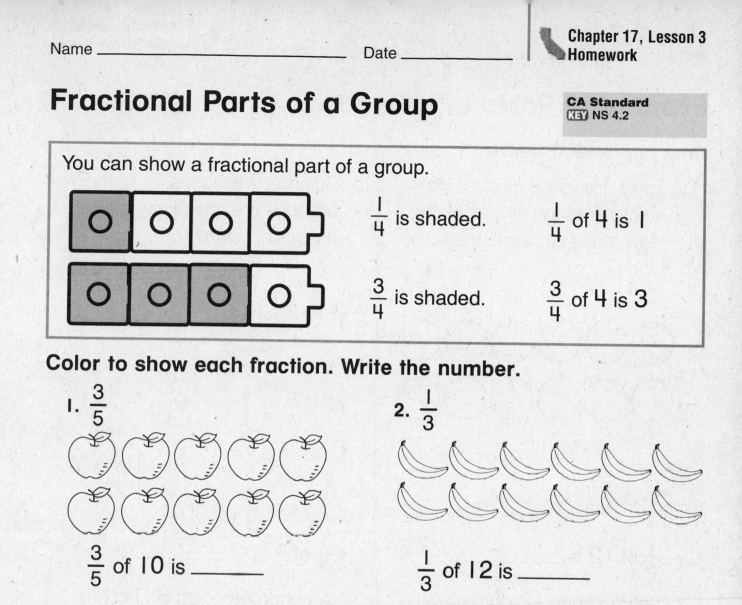

$\frac{1}{4}$ is shaded. $\frac{1}{4}$ of 4 is 1

$\frac{3}{4}$ is shaded. $\frac{3}{4}$ of 4 is 3

Color to show each fraction. Write the number.

1. $\frac{3}{5}$

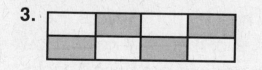

$\frac{3}{5}$ of 10 is _____

2. $\frac{1}{3}$

$\frac{1}{3}$ of 12 is _____

Spiral Review   (Chapter 16, Lesson 3) **KEY NS 4.2, NS 4.0**

Write the fraction for the shaded parts.

3.

4.

_____   _____

Name _____ Date _____

Fractional Parts of a Group

CA Standard
KEY NS 4.2

Draw and color to solve.

1. Jerry draws 12 circles. He colors $\frac{1}{6}$ of the circles black. How many circles are colored black?

⃝⃝⃝⃝⃝⃝
⃝⃝⃝⃝⃝⃝

$\frac{1}{6}$ of 12 is _____

2. Sue has 9 balloons. $\frac{1}{3}$ of the balloons are gray. How many balloons are gray?

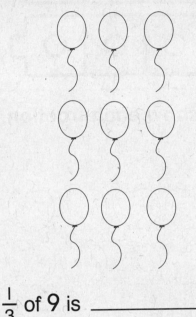

$\frac{1}{3}$ of 9 is _____

3. Lauren buys 12 ribbons. She shares them equally with two friends. How many ribbons does each friend get?

$\frac{1}{3}$ of 12 is _____

4. Amanda received 8 cherries. She shares them equally with her sister. How many cherries does each girl get?

$\frac{1}{2}$ of 8 is _____

5. Joan and Alice share 6 cupcakes equally. Each of them gets one half of the cupcakes. How many cupcakes does each get?

_____

6. Tony has 15 party favors. He gives $\frac{1}{5}$ of them to Angela. How many party favors does Angela receive?

_____

Name _____ Date _____

Draw a Picture

Think!
How many equal parts
are there in all?

CA Standards
KEY NS 4.2, MR 1.2

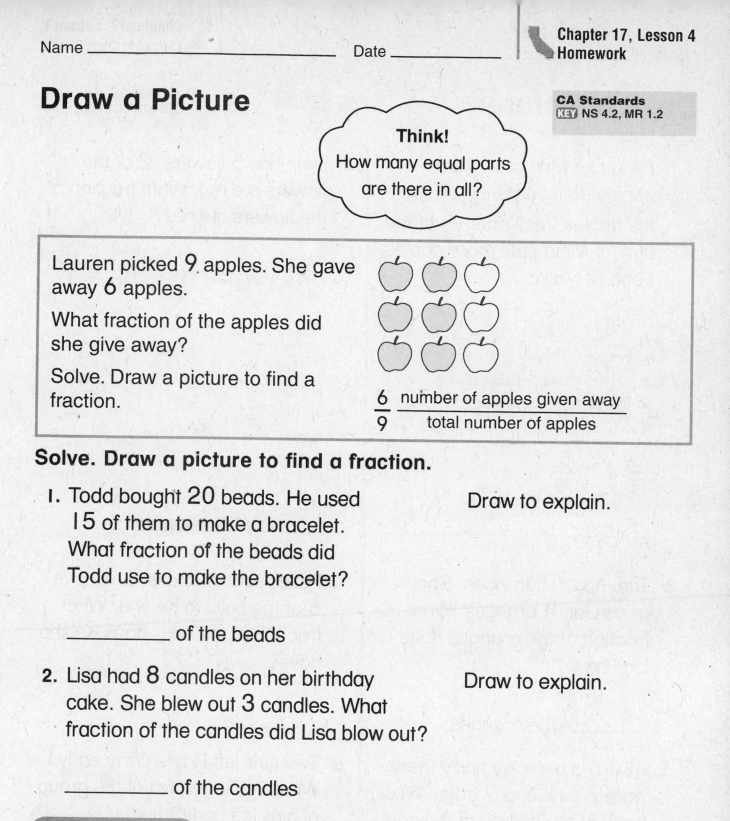

Lauren picked 9 apples. She gave away 6 apples.

What fraction of the apples did she give away?

Solve. Draw a picture to find a fraction.

$\dfrac{6}{9}$ number of apples given away / total number of apples

Solve. Draw a picture to find a fraction.

1. Todd bought 20 beads. He used 15 of them to make a bracelet. What fraction of the beads did Todd use to make the bracelet?

   Draw to explain.

   _____ of the beads

2. Lisa had 8 candles on her birthday cake. She blew out 3 candles. What fraction of the candles did Lisa blow out?

   Draw to explain.

   _____ of the candles

Spiral Review (Chapter 16, Lesson 4) **KEY NS 4.3, KEY NS 4.2**

3. Write the fraction for the shaded parts.

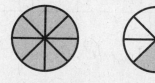

   _____

Draw a Picture

CA Standards
KEY NS 4.2, MR 1.2

1. Feng and Mali picked 18 apples. Feng eats $\frac{3}{18}$ of the apples. Mali eats $\frac{5}{18}$ of the apples. Who eats more apples, Feng or Mali?

$$\frac{3}{18} \bigcirc \frac{5}{18}$$

_____

2. Lynn has 5 flowers. 2 of the flowers are red. What fraction of the flowers are red?

_____ of the flowers

3. Tara has 10 oranges. She gives Lian 4 oranges. What fraction of the oranges does Lian have?

_____ of the oranges

4. Pat bought 12 balls. She gave 6 of the balls to Keisha. What fraction of the balls does Keisha have?

_____

5. At Ray's birthday party there were 8 girls and 9 boys. What fraction of children at the party were boys?

_____

6. Two girls left Ray's party early. What fractional part of the group of girls left early?

_____

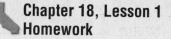
Hands On: Nonstandard Units

CA Standards
MG 1.1, MR 1.2

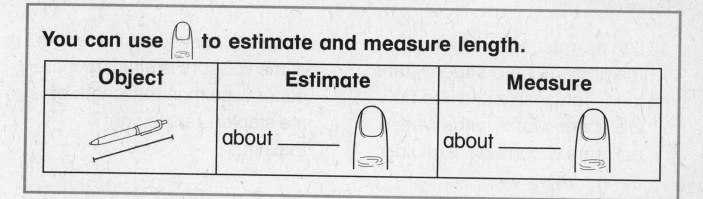

You can use 👆 to estimate and measure length.

Object	Estimate	Measure
(pen)	about _____ 👆	about _____ 👆

Find the real object.
Estimate the length. Use 👆 to measure.

Object	Estimate	Measure
I. (watch)	about _____ 👆	about _____ 👆
2. (spoon)	about _____ 👆	about _____ 👆
3. (shoe)	about _____ 👆	about _____ 👆

Spiral Review (Chapter 17, Lesson 1) **KEY** NS 4.1, MR 1.2

4. Write a fraction to complete the comparison.

_____

_____ > $\frac{1}{2}$ $\frac{1}{3}$ < _____   _____ = _____

Hands On: Nonstandard Units

CA Standards
MG 1.1, MR 1.2

Solve.

1. Jan estimates the length of the string to be 5 finger widths long. Tony estimates it to be 25 finger widths long. Whose estimate is correct? Explain.

   _____

   _____

   _____

2. Maya estimates that the length of the scissors is equal to more paper clips than the length of the stapler. Is she right? Explain.

   _____

3. Tyler wants to measure the length of his desk. Which unit would he use the most of to find the length?

   footprint   paper clip   pencil

4. Ramon wants to measure the length of his pinky finger. Which unit of measure should he use?

   ones cubes   pencils   footprint

5. Todd's lunchbox is 3 finger lengths longer than his pencil case. How many finger lengths will it take to measure his lunchbox if his pencil case measures 5 finger lengths?

   _____ finger lengths

6. Jamie used fingers to measure both pieces of string. If Jamie wanted to make both pieces of string the same length, how much string should he add to the shorter piece?

   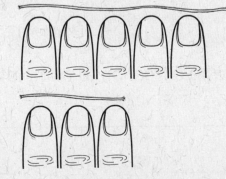

Hands On: Compare Nonstandard Units

CA Standards
MG 1.2, MG 1.1

You can use different units to measure the same object.
You can use different items like paper clips, coins, or blocks that you find in your home or your fingers to measure the pencil.

The pencil is about 5 ⬯ long.

The pencil is about 7 ◻ long.

Find the real object. Measure the length with two different units. Draw the unit that you used to measure.

Object	Measurement
1.	about _____ about _____
2.	about _____ about _____
3.	about _____ about _____
4.	about _____ about _____

Spiral Review (Chapter 17, Lesson 2) **KEY NS 4.2, NS 4.0**

5. Write the fraction.

_____ gray   _____ black

Use with text pp. 353–354

Name _____ Date _____

Hands On: Compare Nonstandard Units

1. Carol measured the length of a paintbrush as 6 paper clips or as 12 ones blocks. How many more ones blocks than paper clips did the paintbrush measure?

_____

2. Look at the units used in exercise 1. What can we say about the size of a paper clip compared to the size of a ones block?

_____

_____

_____

3. Alejandro measured the length of his classroom as 25 footsteps. Gloria measured the same classroom as 35 footsteps. Why were the measurements different?

_____

_____

_____

4. Karen measures the length of her bed using handprints and paper clips. Which unit of measure did she use more of? Why?

_____

_____

_____

5. Joshua used pencils and paper clips to measure the length of his backpack. He knows that one pencil is 4 paper clips long. If his backpack measures 6 pencils long, how many paper clips long is it?

_____ paper clips

6. If Joshua measures the same backpack using ones blocks that are half the size of a paper clip, how many ones blocks long is his backpack?

_____ ones blocks

Use with text pp. 353–354

Hands On: Inches

CA Standards
KEY MG 1.3, NS 6.1

An inch ruler can be used to measure length in inches.

Object	Estimate	Measure
	about 2 inches	about 3 inches

Find the real object.
Estimate. Then measure with a ruler.

Object	Estimate	Measure
1.	about _____ inches	about _____ inches
2.	about _____ inches	about _____ inches
3.	about _____ inches	about _____ inches
4.	about _____ inches	about _____ inches
5.	about _____ inches	about _____ inches

Spiral Review (Chapter 17, Lesson 3) **KEY NS 4.2**

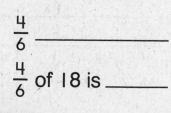

6. Color to show the fraction. Write the number.

$\frac{4}{6}$ _____

$\frac{4}{6}$ of 18 is _____

Use with text pp. 355–356

Inches

CA Standards
KEY MG 1.3, NS 6.1

1. Molly says that this piece of ribbon is 4 inches long. Ben says that the ribbon is 3 inches long. Who is correct?

_____

2. Ben has another piece of ribbon that is 2 inches shorter than the one above. How long is Ben's ribbon?

_____ inches

3. Jonah needs to cut a piece of string that measures 5 inches long. Sarah draws a line to show him how long the string should be. Draw the line that Sarah drew.

_____

_____

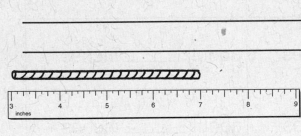

4. Diane, Val, and Indira each have crayons. Diane's crayon is 2 inches long. Val's crayon is twice as long as Diane's. Indira had the longest crayon of all three. Draw and label the length of Indira's crayon.

_____

_____

_____

5. Luan measures her straw and says that it is 6 inches long. What did she do wrong? How long is her straw?

_____

_____

_____

_____

6. Peter has a straw that is half the length of Luan's. Draw a line above the ruler to show the length of Peter's straw.

_____

_____

_____

Hands On: Centimeters

CA Standards
KEY MG 1.3, NS 6.1

You can use a centimeter ruler to measure length in centimeters.

Object	Estimate	Measure
	about 12 cm	about 15 cm

Find the real object.
Estimate. Then use a ruler to measure.

Object	Estimate	Measure
1. Library Card Name :	about _____ cm	about _____ cm
2.	about _____ cm	about _____ cm
3.	about _____ cm	about _____ cm
4.	about _____ cm	about _____ cm

5. Look at the four lengths. Write the names of the objects from shortest to longest.

_____ _____ _____ _____

Spiral Review (Chapter 17, Lesson 3) **KEY NS 4.2**

6. Tony has 5 green markers and 2 red markers. What fraction of the markers is green?

_____ of the markers are green.

Hands On: Centimeters

Solve.

1. Owen measures a spoon with a ruler. About how long is the spoon?

   about 12 cm   about 50 cm

2. Lisa wants to make a pencil case. She needs to measure the length of her pencils. Which unit of measure should she use?

   foot print   cm ruler   pencil

3. Marsha used paper clips to measure the length of her bracelet. She recorded the length as 7 paper clips. She then measured the length of her bracelet in centimeters and recorded it as 14 cm. How many centimeters long were the paper clips Marsha used as units of measure?

   _____ cm

4. Marsha's necklace is two times the length of her bracelet. Draw her necklace and label the length.

5. Magda draws a line 5 cm long. Gina draws a line 5 inches long. Who draws the longer line?

   _____

6. Sandy found a feather that measured 15 centimeters long. Don's feather measured 15 paper clips long. Whose feather is the longest? Explain.

   _____

   _____

   _____

Name _____ Date _____

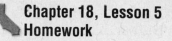
Use Measurement

David wants to add beads to his key chain. He wants the total length to be 9 centimeters. How many centimeters should he add?

Length of key chain: 6 cm

total length − length of key chain = length needed to add

9 cm − 6 cm = 3 cm

Solution: David needs to add 3 cm.

Use the picture to solve the problem.

1. James wants to cut strips of paper the same length as this pencil. How long will each strip of paper be?

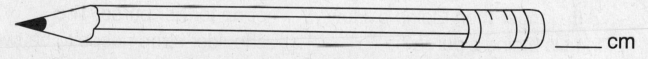

_____ cm

2. Ann measures these bookmarks to the nearest inch. How much longer is the white bookmark than the gray bookmark?

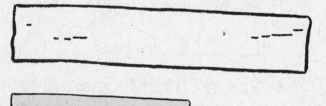

_____ inches

Spiral Review (Chapter 17, Lesson 3) **KEY NS 4.2**

3. Penny has 4 polka dot hair bows and 5 striped hair bows. What fraction of the hair bows has polka dots?

_____ of the hair bows have polka dots.

Name _____ Date _____

Use Measurement

CA Standards
KEY MG 1.3, NS 6.1

Answer the questions. Solve the problem.

1. JoAnn uses squares of material to make a rug for her dollhouse. How many squares does she need to make the rug?

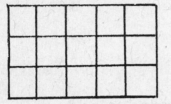

_____ squares

2. Joyce has strips of fabric. What is the total length of the fabric? Explain.

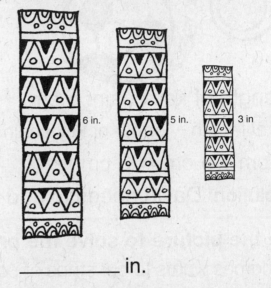

6 in.   5 in.   3 in

_____ in.

3. This is Marlene's purse. It is 3 in. longer than Elaine's. How long is Elaine's purse?

11 in.

_____ inches

4. Elaine wants to make a shoulder strap for her purse. The shoulder strap needs to be two times the length of the purse. How long should Elaine make the shoulder strap?

_____ inches

5. Laura has a ribbon that is 4 inches long and a ribbon that is 6 inches long. How many half-inch pieces can she cut from both ribbons?

_____

6. Ellis is 15 centimeters shorter than Morgan. How tall is Ellis?

Morgan is 125 centimeters tall.

_____ cm

Hands On: Make a Clock and Show Time to the Hour

CA Standard
MG 1.4

Draw hands on the clock to show the time.
five o'clock

hour → 5 : 00 ← minutes after the hour

Draw hands on the clock to show the time. Then write the time.

1. one o'clock

2. eleven o'clock

3. four o'clock

4. two o'clock

_____

_____

_____

_____

5. twelve o'clock

6. three o'clock

7. six o'clock

8. nine o'clock

_____

_____

_____

_____

Spiral Review (Chapter 18, Lesson 1) **MG 1.1, MR 1.2**

9. Use 👆 to measure. Write about how many.

Purple

about _____ 👆

about _____ 👆

Hands On: Make a Clock and Show Time to the Hour

CA Standard
MG 1.4

Solve.

1. Linda wants to leave the house at 4:00. What should the hands on the clock look like when she leaves?

_____

_____

_____

2. Judy's bus leaves at 8 o'clock. She has to get up one hour before that to get ready. What time will she get up?

_____

_____

3. Rita's doctor appointment is at 3:00. Where will the clock hands be at this time?

_____

_____

_____

4. Derek's music class begins at 1:00. He looks at the clock and the hour hand is on the 3. Is he on time or late for his class?

_____

_____

_____

5. Alex has to go to sleep when the minute hand is on the 12 and the hour hand is on the 9. What time does he have to go to sleep?

_____

6. José is allowed to have a snack at 3 o'clock. What number will the minute hand on the clock be touching then?

_____

Time Before and After the Hour

CA Standard
MG 1.4

Skip count by 5s to find the minutes.

Time After the Hour

Time Before the Hour

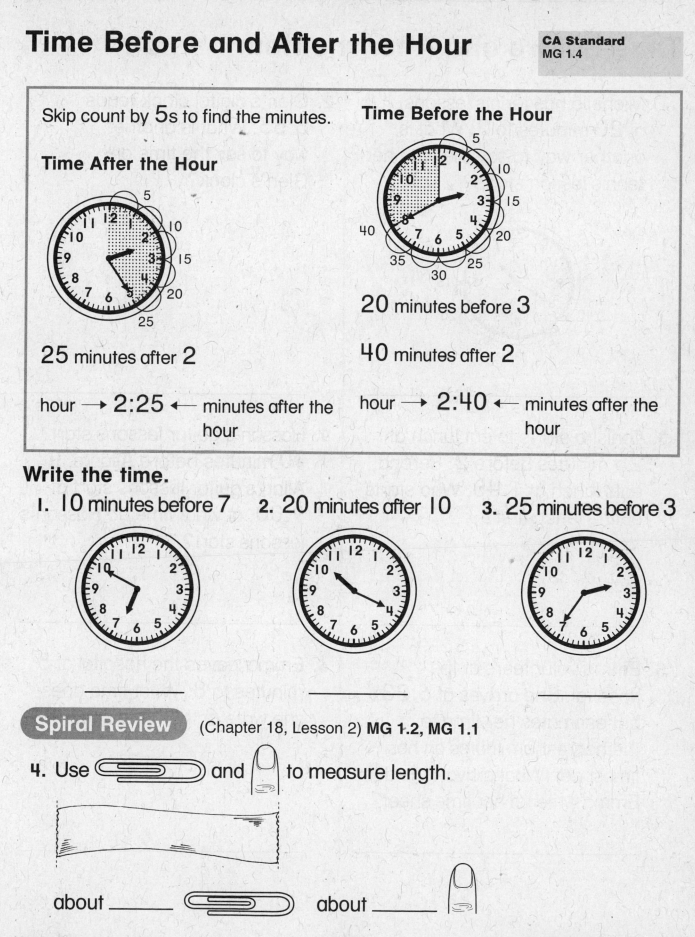

25 minutes after 2

20 minutes before 3

40 minutes after 2

hour → 2:25 ← minutes after the hour

hour → 2:40 ← minutes after the hour

Write the time.

1. 10 minutes before 7

2. 20 minutes after 10

3. 25 minutes before 3

_____   _____   _____

Spiral Review   (Chapter 18, Lesson 2) **MG 1.2, MG 1.1**

4. Use ⬭ and 👍 to measure length.

about _____ ⬭   about _____ 👍

Time Before and After the Hour

CA Standard
MG 1.4

1. Michelle has tennis lessons at 20 minutes to 2. What is another way to say the time her tennis lesson starts?

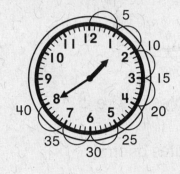

2. Glen's digital clock reads 3:55. What is another way to say the time on Glen's clock?

3. Tanisha starts to eat lunch at 25 minutes before 2. Serena eats lunch at 1:45. Who starts eating lunch first?

4. Hassan's guitar lessons start 10 minutes before Allan's. If Allan's guitar lessons start at 9:00, at what time do Hassan's lessons start?

5. Emma volunteers at the hospital. She arrives at 6:23 but estimates her time to the nearest 5 minutes on her timesheet. What arrival time does Emma write on her time sheet?

6. Emma leaves the hospital at 5 minutes to 8. What time does she write on her time sheet?

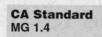
Time to 15 Minutes

CA Standard
MG 1.4

There are **15** minutes in a quarter hour.

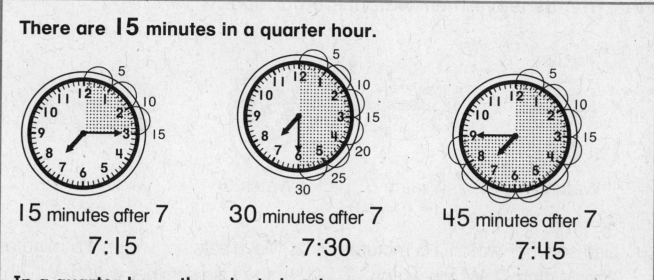

15 minutes after **7**
7:15

30 minutes after **7**
7:30

45 minutes after **7**
7:45

In a quarter hour, the minute hand moves around one fourth of the clock.

Draw the hour and minute hands on the clock to show the time. Write the time.

1. quarter past 3   2. quarter to 5   3. quarter past 6   4. half past 7

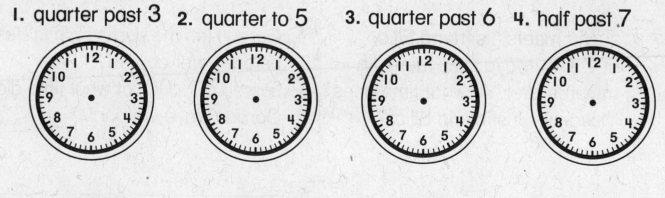

_____   _____   _____   _____

Spiral Review   (Chapter 18, Lesson 3) **KEY** MG 1.3, NS 6.1

Estimate. Then measure with a ruler.

Estimate: about _____ inches

Measure: about _____ inches

Time to 15 Minutes

CA Standard
MG 1.4

Four friends leave their watches on a table.

Watch A

Watch B

Watch C

Watch D

1. Lisa sets her watch 15 minutes after Watch C. Which watch belongs to Lisa?

   Watch _____

2. Maya sets her watch 15 minutes after Lisa sets her watch. Which watch belongs to Maya?

   Watch _____

3. Justin meets his friend Elliot at 2:00. Maya joins them 15 minutes later. At what time does Maya join Justin and Elliot?

   _____

4. Gordan left the party 15 minutes before Peter arrived. If Peter arrived at 6:00, at what time did Gordan leave the party?

   _____

5. Paula and Sam played in the park for 30 minutes. How many quarter hours did they spend in the park?

   _____ quarter hours

6. Todd and Karen start playing chess at 3:00. They play for 3 quarter hours. How many minutes later do they finish playing chess?

   _____ minutes later

Elapsed Time

CA Standard
MG 1.5

| Soccer Practice | | A.M. is used for the time 12 midnight to 12 noon. |
| Start Time | End Time | |

A.M. is used for the time 12 midnight to 12 noon.

P.M. is used for the time from 12 noon to 12 midnight.

11:00 ___ A.M.   1:00 ___ P.M.

The practice lasts

___2___ hours.

Write the times. Then write how much time has passed.

Start Time	End Time	How long does the practice last?
_____ A.M.	_____ P.M.	_____ hours

Spiral Review (Chapter 18, Lesson 4) **KEY** MG 1.3, NS 6.1

Estimate. Then measure with a ruler.

Estimate: about _____ cm

Measure: about _____ cm

Elapsed Time

1. JoAnn goes to the movies. The movie starts at 3:00 P.M. It is over at 5:00 P.M. How long did the movie last?

The movie lasted for

_____ hours.

2. Mario goes to baseball practice at 10:00 A.M. Practice is over at 1:00 P.M. How long does baseball practice last?

Baseball practice lasts for

_____ hours.

3. Howard goes to the park at 11:00 A.M. He stays there for 4 hours. At what time does Howard leave the park?

Howard leaves the park at

_____ P.M.

4. Chris starts reading a book at 2:00 P.M. She reads for 2 hours. At what time does Chris stop reading?

Chris stops reading at

_____ P.M.

5. Kiona helped her mother cook dinner at 4:00. They finish 2 and a half hours later. At what time do they finish cooking?

_____

6. Nadia and Jim rake leaves in the garden. They start at 9:00 and end at 2:00. How many hours did they spend raking leaves?

_____ hours

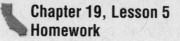

Calendar

**CA Standard
MG 1.4**

A calendar shows the days, weeks, and months in a year.
This calendar shows one month.

December

Sunday	Monday	Tuesday	Wednesday	Thursday	Friday	Saturday
						1
2	3	4	5	6	7	8
9	10	11	12	13	14	15
16	17	18	19	20	21	22
23	24	25	26	27	28	29
30	31					

Use the calendar to answer the questions.

1. On what day of the week does the month begin? _____

2. What is the date of the third Sunday? _____

3. On what day of the week did November end? _____

Circle the longer amount of time.

4. 1 month   10 weeks   5. 3 months   1 year

Circle the shorter amount of time.

6. 3 months   2 weeks   7. 3 days   1 week

Spiral Review (Chapter 18, Lesson 4) **KEY MG 1.3, NS 6.1**

6. Which is longer 5 cm or 5 inches? Explain.

_____

Calendar

CA Standard
MG 1.4

1. It takes Ramon 1 week to paint the doghouse. It takes him 10 days to teach the dog to roll over. Which activity takes longer?

_____

_____

2. Alison's birthday will be in 3 weeks. Matt's birthday will be in 10 days. Whose birthday will be first?

_____ birthday

3. Juan goes to sleep-away camp for the whole summer. Circle the amount of time that he might be at camp.

2 weeks   2 days   2 months

4. How many hours are in 2 days?

_____ hours

5. Paula's birthday is Tuesday, June 1st. Dora's birthday is the day before. What is the day and date of Dora's birthday?

_____

6. Jim's birthday is exactly 2 weeks after Dora's birthday. What is the day and date of Jim's birthday?

_____

Name _____ Date _____

Use a Table

Information you need to solve a problem can be in a table.

Sergio goes to three after-school activities.

How long does he spend at soccer practice?

Activity	Time
Soccer	3:00–3:30
Drama Club	4:00–5:00
Art Club	5:00–5:30

_30_ minutes

Use the table and a clock to help you solve the problems.

1. Bernard leaves for soccer practice at 2:30. He arrives on time. How long does it take him to get there? _____

2. Lino spends all of his Drama Club time painting scenery. How long does Lino paint scenery? _____

3. Angela is a member of Drama Club. Elisa is a member of the Art Club. Who spends more time at a club? _____

4. Amit goes to the Drama Club and Art Club. How long will he be at both clubs? _____

Spiral Review (Chapter 18, Lesson 5) **KEY** MG 1.3, MR 2.0

5. Marsha wants to add beads to her necklace. She wants the total length to be 16 inches. How many inches should she add?

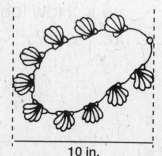

10 in.

_____

Use a Table

Subject	Time
Science	9:00 – 10:00
Reading	10:15 – 11:30
Lunch	11:30 – 12:30
Math	12:45 – 2:15
Art	2:20 – 3:30

1. Lisa agreed to meet Sue right after science class. At what time does science class end?

_____

2. Sue had to go to reading class after meeting Lisa. At what time does reading class start?

_____

3. Malcom wanted to finish his math homework after lunch and hand it in at the beginning of math class. How much time does Malcom have to finish his math homework?

_____

4. Pearl was 30 minutes late for lunch. How much time did she have left to finish her lunch?

_____

5. This year, art class is 10 minutes longer than it was last year. How long was art class last year?

_____

6. Mr. Grover uses the time between classes and after lunch to grade papers. How much time does Mr. Grover spend during the school day grading papers?

_____

Hands On: Equal Groups

CA Standards
KEY NS 3.1, MR 1.2

There are 3 groups of 2. How many in all?
You can add equal groups. $2 + 2 + 2 = 6$
There are 2 in each group.

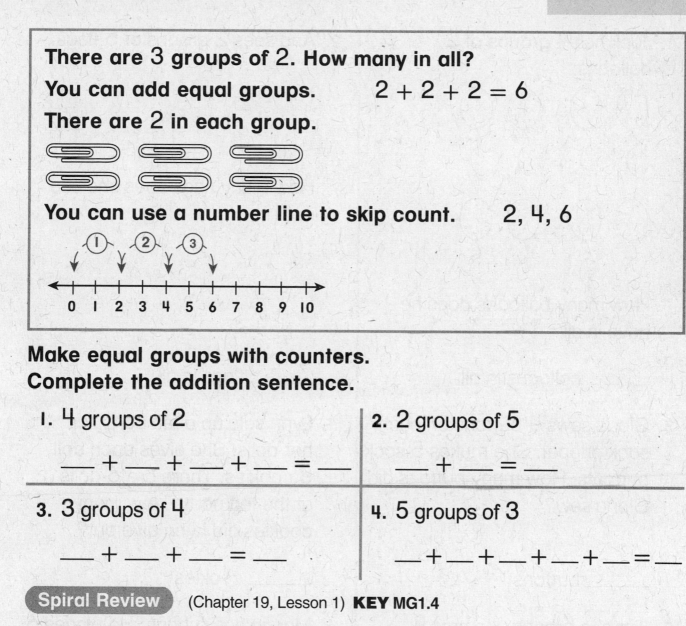

You can use a number line to skip count.   2, 4, 6

Make equal groups with counters.
Complete the addition sentence.

1. 4 groups of 2

___ + ___ + ___ + ___ = ___

2. 2 groups of 5

___ + ___ = ___

3. 3 groups of 4

___ + ___ + ___ = ___

4. 5 groups of 3

___ + ___ + ___ + ___ + ___ = ___

Spiral Review   (Chapter 19, Lesson 1) **KEY** MG1.4

Draw the hands on the clock to show
the time. Then write the time.

5. 7 o'clock

_____

6. 3 o'clock

_____

Use with text pp. 395–396

Hands On: Equal Groups

CA Standards
KEY NS 3.1, MR 1.2

1. Jack has 4 groups of 2 balloons.

How many balloons does he have in all?

_____ balloons in all

2. Ana sees 2 groups of 5 flags.

How many flags does she see in all?

_____ flags in all

3. Gloria sews 4 buttons on each sock puppet. She makes 5 sock puppets. How many buttons did Gloria sew?

_____ buttons

4. Lynn sets up a tea party for her dolls. She gives each doll 3 cookies. There are 6 dolls at the tea party. How many cookies did Lynn give out?

_____ cookies

5. Jim has 5 bags. He puts 4 marbles in each bag. If Jim decides that he wants to have 4 bags but still use the total number of marbles, how many marbles will he put into each of the 4 bags?

_____ marbles

6. Marvin has 6 bags. He places 6 marbles in each bag. How many more marbles does Marvin have than Jim?

_____ more marbles

Arrays

CA Standards
KEY NS 3.1, **KEY** NS 3.0

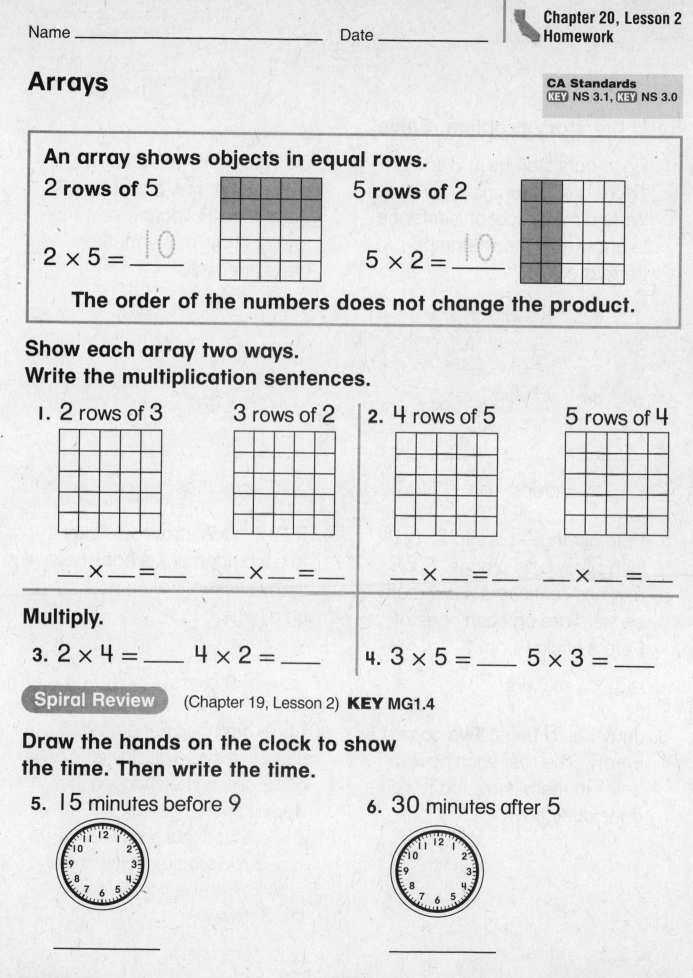

An array shows objects in equal rows.

2 rows of 5

$2 \times 5 = \underline{10}$

5 rows of 2

$5 \times 2 = \underline{10}$

The order of the numbers does not change the product.

Show each array two ways.
Write the multiplication sentences.

1. 2 rows of 3   3 rows of 2

__ × __ = __   __ × __ = __

2. 4 rows of 5   5 rows of 4

__ × __ = __   __ × __ = __

Multiply.

3. $2 \times 4 = \underline{\hspace{1cm}}$ $4 \times 2 = \underline{\hspace{1cm}}$

4. $3 \times 5 = \underline{\hspace{1cm}}$ $5 \times 3 = \underline{\hspace{1cm}}$

Spiral Review   (Chapter 19, Lesson 2) **KEY** MG1.4

**Draw the hands on the clock to show
the time. Then write the time.**

5. 15 minutes before 9

6. 30 minutes after 5

_____   _____

Arrays

Read the story problem. Solve.

CA Standards
KEY NS 3.1, **KEY** NS 3.0

1. Rose puts stamps in 3 rows. There are 5 stamps in 3 rows. Write a multiplication sentence to show how many stamps there are.

   _____ × _____ = _____

   _____ stamps

2. Carl puts 5 rows of muffins in a box. Each row has 4 muffins. Write a multiplication sentence to show how many muffins there are in all.

   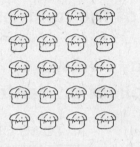

   _____ × _____ = _____

   _____ muffins

3. Pete arranges his sticker book with 5 rows on a page. Each row has 5 stickers. How many stickers are on each page of Pete's sticker book?

   _____ stickers

4. If Pete adds a row of stickers to each page of his book how many stickers will he now have on a page?

   _____ stickers

5. Judy has 5 bags. Two bags are empty. The rest each have 5 coins in them. How many coins does Judy have in all?

   _____ coins

6. Abbie arranged her eraser collection into a display of 2 rows of 12. Then she changed the display into 6 rows of 4. Finally, she decided that she liked the way 3 rows looked. How many erasers did she have in each of the 3 rows?

   _____ erasers

Hands On: Skip Counting to Multiply

CA Standards
KEY NS 3.1, KEY NS 3.0

There are 10 cubes in each cube train.
How many cubes are in 3 trains?

$3 \times 10 = \underline{30}$

____, ____, ____
10, 20, 30

Solution:
There are __30__ cubes in 3 trains.

**Draw cube trains. Skip count.
Then find the product.**

1. 5 trains of 10 cubes

____, ____, ____, ____, ____

$5 \times 10 =$ _____ cubes in all

2. 7 trains of 5 cubes

___, ___, ___, ___, ___, ___, ___

$7 \times 5 =$ _____ cubes in all

Multiply.

3. $7 \times 2 =$ _____

4. $3 \times 3 =$ _____

5. $6 \times 5 =$ _____

Spiral Review (Chapter 19, Lesson 3) **KEY** MG 1.4

**Draw the hands on the clock to show
the time. Then write the time.**

6. half past 8

7. quarter to 1

_____

_____

Name _____ Date _____

Hands On: Skip Counting to Multiply

CA Standards
KEY NS 3.1, KEY NS 3.0

1. Devin uses 4 blocks to make each tower. He makes 3 towers. Skip count to find how many blocks Devin uses in all.

   _____, _____, _____

   _____ blocks

2. Kelsey uses 10 beads to make each bracelet. She makes 6 bracelets. Skip count to find how many beads Kelsey uses in all.

   _____, _____, _____, _____,

   _____, _____ beads

3. Jenna makes 5 ice cream sundaes. She puts 3 cherries on each ice cream sundae. How many cherries does Jenna use?

   _____ cherries

4. Mr. Avilo packs boxes of candles. He packs 10 boxes. Each box contains 10 candles. How many candles does Mr. Avilo pack altogether?

   _____ candles

5. Simon bought 6 and one half boxes of donuts for his class party. Each whole box contains 10 donuts. How many donuts did Simon bring to his class?

   _____ donuts

6. Chris brought grapes to her class party. There are 5 grapes on each stem. There is a stem for each of the 12 people in the class. How many grapes are there in all?

   _____ grapes

Name _____ Date _____

Use Tables to Multiply

Janice has 3 teacups. She puts 2 sugar cubes in each teacup.

How many sugar cubes are there?

Skip count by 2s.

2, 4, 6

Solution: There are 6 sugar cubes.

teacups	1	2	3
sugar cubes	2	4	6

Skip count to complete the table.
Write the multiplication sentence to solve.

1. Ira has 4 letters. Each letter has 3 stamps. How many stamps does he have?

letters	1	2	3	4
stamps				

_____

___ × ___ = ___

2. Pat bought 5 blueberry muffins. Each muffin has 10 blueberries. How many blueberries are there in all?

muffins	1	2	3	4	5
blueberries					

_____

___ × ___ = ___

3. Paul bought 5 packs of pencils. There are 6 pencils in each pack. How many pencils did he buy?

_____

Spiral Review (Chapter 19, Lesson 4) **KEY** MG 1.5

4. A movie runs from 11:00 A.M. to 1:30 P.M. How long is the movie?

5. Abby starts school at 9:00. She eats lunch at 12:00. How long are her morning classes?

_____ _____

Use with text pp. 401–402

Use Tables to Multiply

CA Standards
KEY NS 3.1, SDAP 2.1

1. Carla knits 10 rows of her sweater every night. How many rows does she knit in 3 nights?

Night	1	2	3
Rows			

_____ rows

2. Earl collects shells at the beach. He collects 5 shells every hour. How many shells does Earl collect in 4 hours?

Night	1	2	3	4
Rows				

_____ shells

3. Mary reads 20 pages each day. How many days will it take her to read 100 pages?

_____ days

4. Chen completes 5 homework problems in 1 hour. How many hours will it take him to complete 20 homework problems?

_____ hours

5. Hiro completes twice as many problems in the same amount of time as Chen. How long will it take him to complete 20 homework problems?

_____ hours

6. Yusef writes 2 pages each day in his journal. His journal has 60 pages. How long will it take Yusef to fill all of the pages in his journal?

_____ days

Problem Solving Field Trip

CA Standards
KEY NS 3.1, NS 3.0

Choose the correct answer. Show your work.

1. Jeffery keeps his collection of arrowheads in
6 boxes. He keeps 5 arrowheads in each box.
How many arrowheads has Jeffery collected?

   11   25   30   41

2. Ralph displays his fossil collection in 3 glass cases.
Each case contains 3 fossils. How many fossils does
Ralph display?

   12   9   6   3

3. Mina and three of her friends collect mineral samples.
So far, they have each collected 6 samples. How
many samples do they have altogether?

   _____

4. Mina and her three friends collect a few more
samples. They add them to their earlier collection
and display all of the samples in 5 glass cases. There
are 6 samples in each case. How many new samples
were added to the collection?

   _____

Spiral Review (Chapter 19, Lesson 5) **KEY MG1.4**

5. Circle the longer amount of
time.

   2 weeks   12 days

6. Circle the shorter amount of
time.

   2 hours   90 minutes

Use with text pp. 403–404

Problem Solving Field Trip

CA Standard
KEY NS 3.1, NS 3.0

1. The museum shows a Digging for Fossils movie. Each movie showing holds 10 children. How many children will see the movie by the 4th showing?

Movie showing	1	2	3	4
Number of Children				

_____ children

2. The tables in the museum cafeteria are arranged in 5 rows with 4 tables in each row. How many tables are in the cafeteria?

_____ tables

3. Mr. Cane's class sits at 3 tables in the cafeteria. There are 6 children at each table. How many children are in Mr. Cane's class?

_____ children

4. The cafeteria staff gives each of the children in Mr. Cane's class 2 pieces of fruit. How many pieces of fruit in all did the staff give out?

_____ pieces of fruit

5. The museum director calculated that 50 children enter the museum every hour. How many children have entered the museum at the end of an 8-hour day?

_____ children

6. Before leaving the museum Mrs. James checks that all of her students are present. She arranges the children into 3 groups of 5 and 3 groups of 3. How many children did Mrs. James take to the museum?

_____ children

Hands On: Multiply in Any Order

CA Standards
KEY NS 3.1, KEY AF 1.1,
MR 3.0

You can multiply in any order and get the same product.

2 rows of 5

5 rows of 2

$2 \times 5 =$ _____ 10

$5 \times 2 =$ _____ 10

The order of the numbers does not change the product.

Color to make the arrays. Find each product.

1. 2 rows of 3   3 rows of 2

$2 \times 3 =$ ___ $3 \times 2 =$ ___

2. 4 rows of 5   5 rows of 4

$4 \times 5 =$ ___ $5 \times 4 =$ ___

Multiply.

3. $2 \times 4 =$ ___ $4 \times 2 =$ ___

4. $3 \times 5 =$ ___ $5 \times 3 =$ ___

5. $1 \times 3 =$ ___ $3 \times 1 =$ ___

6. $6 \times 2 =$ ___ $2 \times 6 =$ ___

Spiral Review (Chapter 20, Lesson 1) **KEY** NS 3.1, MR 1.2

Make equal groups with counters.
Complete the addition sentence.

7. 3 groups of 3

___ + ___ + ___ = ___

8. 4 groups of 5

___ + ___ + ___ + ___ = ___

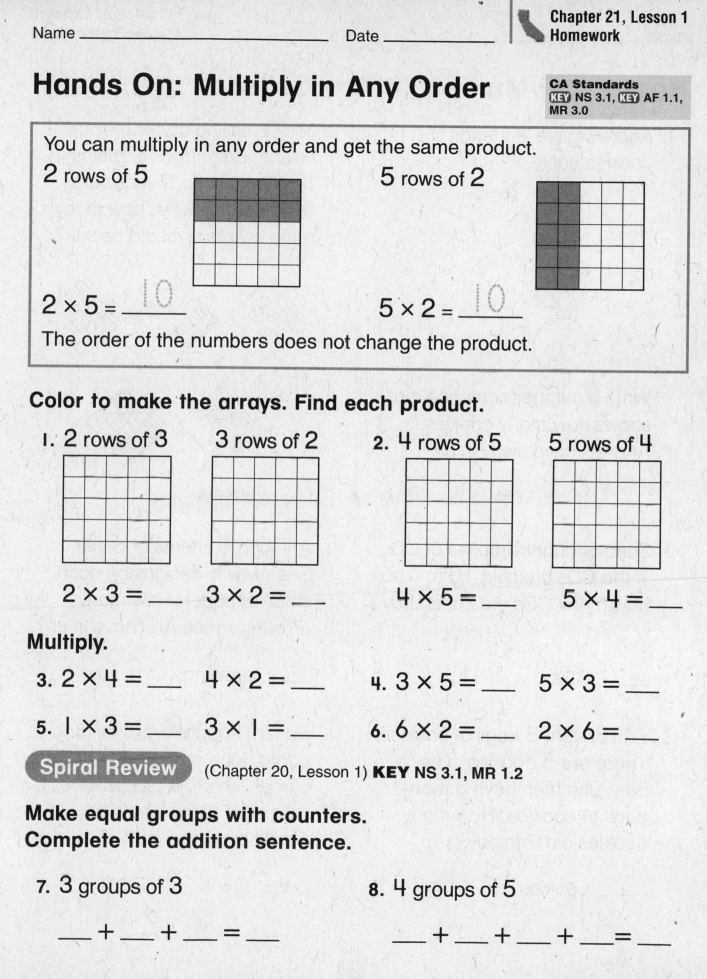

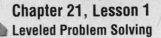
Hands On: Multiply in Any Order

CA Standards
KEY AF 1.1, **KEY** NS 3.1,
MR 3.0

1. Andrew gave 2 friends 3 cookies each.

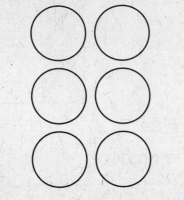

Write a number sentence that shows how many cookies Andrew gave away in all.

_____ × _____ = _____

2. Jack is selling books of raffle tickets. Each book contains 5 raffle tickets. If Jack sells 5 books of tickets, how many raffle tickets in all did he sell?

_____ tickets

3. Zariah bought 3 boxes of CDs. If the CDs are sold 10 to a box, how many CDs did Zariah buy?

_____ CDs

4. Ann had 6 sheets of paper. She drew 4 designs on each sheet of paper. How many drawings does Ann have in all?

_____ drawings

5. Erin bought 3 bags of cookies. There are 5 cookies in each bag. She then buys 3 more bags of cookies. How many cookies did Erin buy?

_____ cookies

6. Sandra bought 8 pizzas for a party. Each pizza is cut into 8 pieces. 3 of the pizzas were pepperoni. How many slices were not pepperoni?

_____ slices

Multiply by 2

CA Standards
KEY NS 3.3, KEY NS 3.1

You can add equal groups to find the sum.
You can multiply equal groups to find the product.

4 groups of 2

Add:

$2 + 2 + 2 + 2 = \underline{8}$

Multiply.

$4 \quad \times \quad 2 \quad = \quad \underline{8}$

number of   number in   product
groups   each group

Find the sum. Then find the product.

1. 5 groups of 2

$2 + 2 + 2 + 2 + 2 = \underline{}$

$5 \times 2 = \underline{}$

2. 3 groups of 2

$2 + 2 + 2 = \underline{}$

$3 \times 2 = \underline{}$

3. $8 \times 2 = \underline{}$

4. $1 \times 2 = \underline{}$

Spiral Review   (Chapter 20, Lesson 2) **KEY** NS 3.1, **KEY** NS 3.0

Show the array 2 ways. Write the multiplication sentences.

5. 3 rows of 4   4 rows of 3

$\underline{} \times \underline{} = \underline{}$

$\underline{} \times \underline{} = \underline{}$

Homework
207
Use with text pp. 413–414

Multiply by 2

CA Standards
KEY NS 3.3, **KEY** NS 3.1

1. Sharon pours 3 glasses of lemonade for her friends. She puts 2 ice cubes in each glass. How many ice cubes does Sharon use?

_____ ice cubes

2. Jim sets the table for 8 people. He places 2 spoons at each place setting. How many spoons did Jim set out?

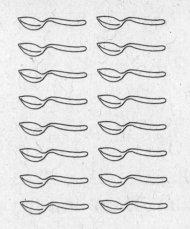

_____ spoons

3. Doris will receive 2 stickers for every book she read over the summer. If Doris read 10 books, how many stickers can she expect to receive?

_____ stickers

4. Paul brushes his teeth 2 times a day. How many times does he brush his teeth in 7 days?

_____ times

4. Oscar has 6 Cub Scout shirts. There are 5 badges on each shirt. 2 of the badges on each shirt are red. How many red badges does Oscar have?

_____ red badges

5. Tyrone went fishing with his grandfather. For every hour he was at the lake Tyrone caught 2 fish. How many fish did Tyrone have when they left for home 8 hours later?

_____ fish

Use with text pp. 413–414

Multiply by 5

CA Standards
KEY NS 3.3, KEY NS 3.1

There are 5 marbles in each bag.
How many marbles are there in all?
You can skip count by 5s to add.

__5__ + __5__ + __5__ = __15__

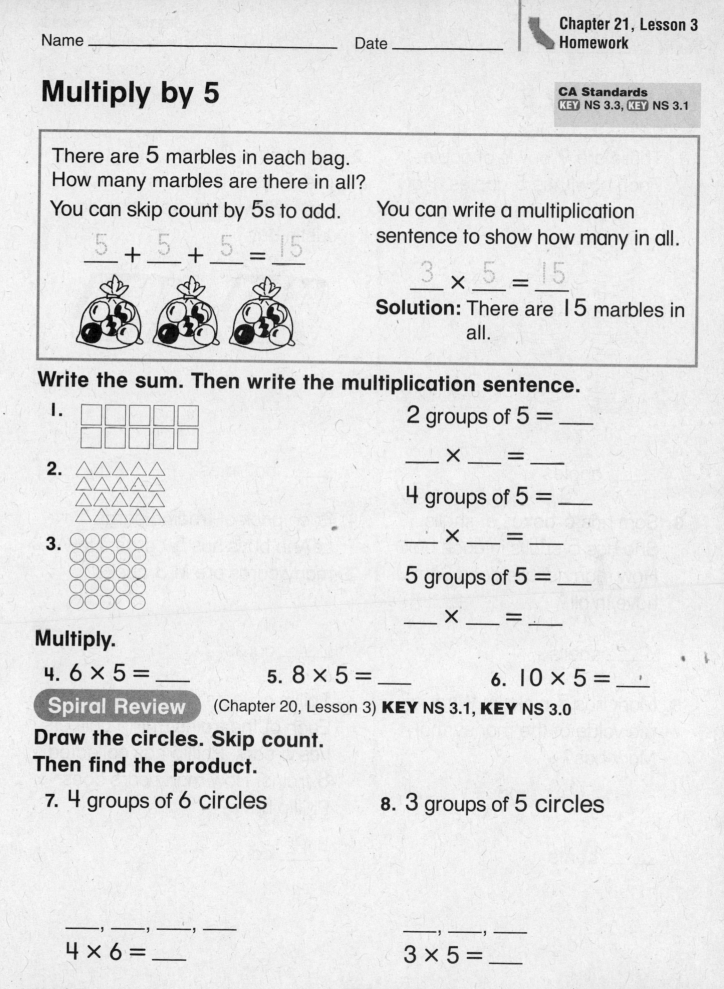

You can write a multiplication sentence to show how many in all.

__3__ × __5__ = __15__

Solution: There are 15 marbles in all.

Write the sum. Then write the multiplication sentence.

1.

2 groups of 5 = ___

___ × ___ = ___

2.

4 groups of 5 = ___

___ × ___ = ___

3.

5 groups of 5 = ___

___ × ___ = ___

Multiply.

4. 6 × 5 = ___   5. 8 × 5 = ___   6. 10 × 5 = ___

Spiral Review (Chapter 20, Lesson 3) **KEY** NS 3.1, **KEY** NS 3.0

Draw the circles. Skip count.
Then find the product.

7. 4 groups of 6 circles

8. 3 groups of 5 circles

___, ___, ___, ___

4 × 6 = ___

___, ___, ___

3 × 5 = ___

Name _____ Date _____

Multiply by 5

CA Standards
KEY NS 3.3, KEY NS 3.1

1. There are 9 bowls of apples. Each bowl has 5 apples. How many apples are there in all?

_____ apples

2. Justin buys 2 packs of batteries. There are 5 batteries in each pack. How many batteries does Justin buy?

_____ batteries

3. Sam has 6 boxes of shells. She has 5 shells in each box. How many shells does Sam have in all?

_____ shells

4. Each pack of trading cards LeAnn buys has 5 cards. How many cards are in 3 packs?

_____ cards

5. Mark has 7 nickels. What is the value of the money that Mark has?

_____ cents

6. Phillip collects model trains. Each of the trains Phillip collects has 5 cars. Phillip has collected 8 trains. How many cars does Phillip have?

_____ cars

Multiply by 10

CA Standards
KEY NS 3.3, **KEY** NS 3.1

There are 10 grapes in each bunch.
How many grapes are in 6 bunches?

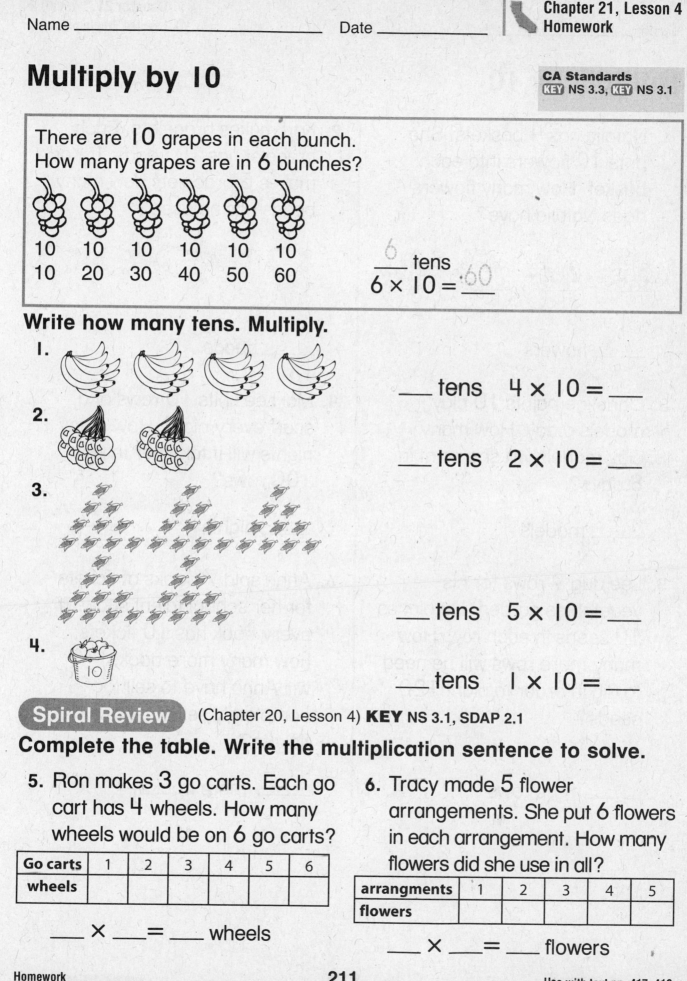

| 10 | 10 | 10 | 10 | 10 | 10 |
| 10 | 20 | 30 | 40 | 50 | 60 |

$\frac{6}{}$ tens

$6 \times 10 = \underline{60}$

Write how many tens. Multiply.

1. ___ tens $4 \times 10 = $ ___

2. ___ tens $2 \times 10 = $ ___

3. ___ tens $5 \times 10 = $ ___

4. ___ tens $1 \times 10 = $ ___

Spiral Review (Chapter 20, Lesson 4) **KEY** NS 3.1, SDAP 2.1

Complete the table. Write the multiplication sentence to solve.

5. Ron makes 3 go carts. Each go cart has 4 wheels. How many wheels would be on 6 go carts?

Go carts	1	2	3	4	5	6
wheels						

___ × ___ = ___ wheels

6. Tracy made 5 flower arrangements. She put 6 flowers in each arrangement. How many flowers did she use in all?

arrangements	1	2	3	4	5
flowers					

___ × ___ = ___ flowers

Multiply by 10

CA Standards
KEY NS 3.3, **KEY** NS 3.1

1. Natalia has 4 baskets. She puts 10 flowers into each basket. How many flowers does Natalia have?

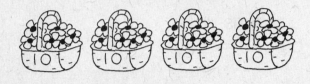

_____ flowers

2. Karl makes bracelets. Each bracelet has 10 beads. If Karl makes 5 bracelets how many beads has he used?

_____ beads

3. Christine paints 10 clay models a day. How many clay models will she paint in 8 days?

_____ models

4. Mai Lee knits 10 rows of a scarf every night. How many nights will it take her to knit 100 rows?

_____ nights

5. Lee dug 9 rows for his vegetables garden. He places 10 seeds in each row. How many more rows will he need to dig in order to plant 120 seeds?

_____ more rows

6. Anna sold 7 books of tickets for her school talent show. If every book has 10 tickets, how many more books will Anna have to sell too completely sell out 150 tickets?

_____ more books

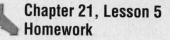
Write a Number Sentence

CA Standards
KEY NS 3.0, KEY NS 3.3

Ms. Vasquez gave pizza slices to 4 children. She gave each child 2 slices. How many pizza slices did she give out in all?

Write a number sentence. Then solve.

__4__ × __2__ = __8__

Ms. Vasquez gave out __8__ pizza slices.

Write a number sentence.
Then solve. Draw or write to explain.

1. Emily drew 6 flowers. Each flower had 5 petals. How many petals did she draw in all?

   ___ × ___ = ___

   ___ petals

2. There were 20 children at a party. The children were put into 5 equal groups to play a game. How many children were in each group?

   ___ × ___ = ___

   ___ children

3. Tom bought 4 bunches of bananas at the store. There were 4 bananas in each bunch. How many bananas did he buy in all?

   ___ × ___ = ___

   ___ bananas

Spiral Review (Chapter 20, Lesson 5) **KEY** NS 3.1, NS 3.0

Solve.

4. The museum displayed its most recent collection of minerals in 5 display cases. Each display case held 8 minerals. How many minerals were displayed? _____

5. The museum added another display case with 8 minerals. How many minerals are displayed now? _____

Use with text pp. 419–422

Name _____ Date _____

Write a Number Sentence

CA Standards
KEY NS 3.0, KEY NS 3.3

1. Ruth buys 2 new sewing kits. There are 5 spools of thread in each kit. How many spools of thread did Ruth buy?

   ____ × 5 = ____

   _____ spools of thread

2. The school auditorium has 10 rows. Each row has 10 seats. How many seats are in the auditorium?

   10 × 10 = ____

   _____ seats

3. Steven buys a box of markers. There are 10 markers in each box. If Steven needed 20 markers how many more boxes does he need to buy?

   ____ × ____ = ____

   _____ box

4. Danny takes the bus to school. The bus has 10 rows with 4 seats in each row. How many seats does the school bus have?

   ____ × ____ = ____

   _____ seats

5. Tennis balls come 4 in each tube. Leon buys 6 tubes. John buys 8 tubes. How many more tennis balls does John buy than Leon?

   ____ × ____ = ____

   ____ × ____ = ____

   ____ − ____ = ____

   _____ more

6. Leslie squeezes 5 lemons into each of 4 jugs. Serena and Tom do the same thing. How many lemons do they all use?

   ____ × ____ = ____

   ____ × ____ = ____

   _____ lemons

Use with text pp. 419–422

Hands On: Equal Groups

CA Standards
KEY NS 3.2, **KEY** NS 3.0

Use 12 beans or other objects and 3 bowls. Divide 12 objects into 3 equal groups.

_____ objects in each bowl. 12 divided into 3 groups is 4.

$12 \div 3 = \underline{\quad 4 \quad}$

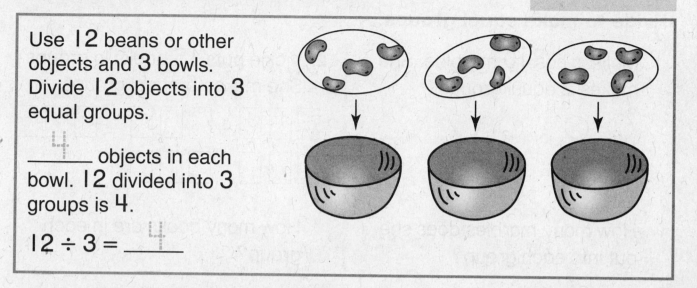

Use objects and bowls. Divide.

1. 10 objects

2 groups

$10 \div 2 = \underline{\qquad}$

_____ in each group

2. 8 objects

4 groups

$8 \div 4 = \underline{\qquad}$

_____ in each group

3. 12 objects

2 groups

$12 \div 2 = \underline{\qquad}$

_____ in each group

4. 9 objects

3 groups

$9 \div 3 = \underline{\qquad}$

_____ in each group

Spiral Review   (Chapter 21, Lesson 1) **KEY AF 1.1, KEY NS 3.1, MR 3.0**

Color to show your work. Find each product.

5. 3 rows of 2

$3 \times 2 = \underline{\qquad}$

2 rows of 3

$2 \times 3 = \underline{\qquad}$

Hands On: Equal Groups

CA Standards
KEY NS 3.2, **KEY** NS 3.0

Divide to make equal groups.

1. Melissa has 10 marbles. She makes 2 equal groups.

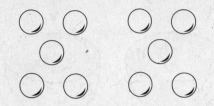

How many marbles does she put into each group?

_____ marbles in each group

2. Vickie puts 15 books in groups. She makes 5 equal groups.

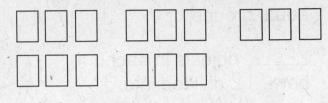

How many books are in each group?

_____ books in each group

3. Billy puts 14 model planes into boxes. 2 model planes fit in each box. How many boxes does Billy need?

_____ boxes

4. Val paints 6 clay mugs. She wants to give pairs of mugs as gifts. How many gifts can she give?

_____ gifts

5. Padama had 6 boxes of shells. There are 3 shells in each box. She wants to give each friend 2 shells. How many friends can Padama give shells to?

_____ friends

6. Matt has 20 yo-yos. He wants to make equal groups. How many equal groups can Matt make?

_____ yo-yos

Equal Groups

CA Standards
KEY NS 3.2, KEY NS 3.0

When you share equally, you divide.
A division sentence tells how many equal groups there are.

Step 1
Start with 6.

Step 2
Subtract groups of 2 until none are left.

$6 - 2 - 2 - 2 = 0$

Step 3
Write how many groups.

divided by

$6 \div 2 = \underline{\ \ 3\ \ }$

groups. 6 divided by 2 equals 3.

Circle equal groups of 2.
Divide. Write the number of groups.

1.

$12 \div 2 = \underline{\ \ \ \ \ }$ groups

2.

$10 \div 2 = \underline{\ \ \ \ \ }$ groups

3.

$8 \div 2 = \underline{\ \ \ \ \ }$ groups

4.

$6 \div 2 = \underline{\ \ \ \ \ }$ groups

Spiral Review (Chapter 21, Lesson 2) **KEY** NS 3.3, **KEY** NS 3.1

Find the sum. Then find the product.

5. 5 groups of 2

$2 + 2 + 2 + 2 + 2 = \underline{\ \ \ \ \ }$

$5 \times 2 = \underline{\ \ \ \ \ }$

Use with text pp. 431–432

Equal Groups

CA Standards
KEY NS 3.2, KEY NS 3.0

1. 2 people share 12 apples equally. How many apples does each person get?

_____ apples

2. 2 children share a bag of 16 peanuts equally. How many peanuts does each child get?

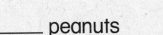

_____ peanuts

3. Richard collected 18 model cars. He keeps 2 cars in each box. How many boxes of model cars does Richard have?

_____ boxes

4. Gloria won 10 marbles. She divided them into 2 equal groups and put them into 2 bags. How many marbles are in each bag?

_____ marbles

5. Louise bought 30 flowers. She wants to create 2 bouquets of equal size for her mother and grandmother. How many flowers should Louise put into each bouquet?

_____ flowers

6. Elise had 10 half-dollar coins. She divided the number of coins into 2 equal groups and donated one group of coins to charity. How much money did Elise donate?

_____

_____

Repeated Subtraction

CA Standards
KEY NS 3.0, KEY NS 3.2

You can use repeated subtraction to divide.
Divide $30 \div 5$.

Step ①
Start at 30

Step ②
Subtract 5s until you have 0.

Step ③
Count how many times you subtracted 5.
I subtracted 5 six times.
$30 \div 5 = \underline{6}$

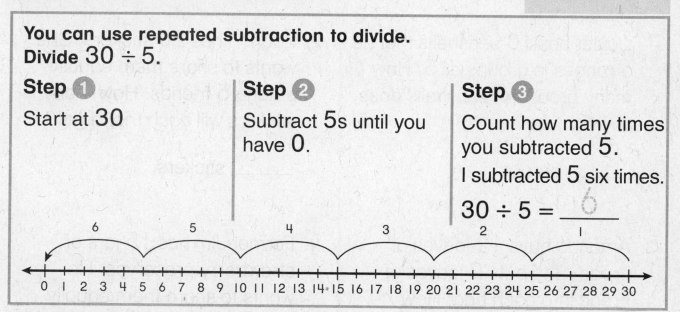

Subtract by 2s to divide by 2.
Use the number line above to divide.

1.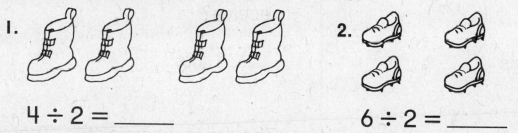

$4 \div 2 = \underline{}$

2.

$6 \div 2 = \underline{}$

Solve. Draw or write to explain.

3. Mark has 12 marbles. He puts them in groups of 2 marbles. How many groups of 2 does he make?

_____ groups

Spiral Review (Chapter 21, Lesson 3) **KEY** NS 3.3, **KEY** NS 3.1

Write how many in all.
Then write the multiplication sentence.

4.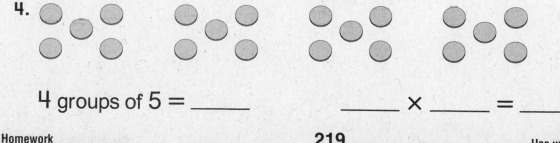

4 groups of 5 = _____   _____ × _____ = _____

Use with text pp. 433–434

Name _____ Date _____

Repeated Subtraction

1. Javier has 10 seashells that he arranges in groups of 5. How many groups of seashells does Javier make?

_____ groups

2. Soon Yi has 20 stickers. She wants to share them equally among 5 friends. How many stickers will each friend get?

_____ stickers

3. Amanda buys 12 loaves of bread. She puts 2 loaves of bread into each bag. How many bags does Amanda have?

_____ bags

4. Farmer Jim has 15 jars of strawberry preserves. He wants to share them equally among 5 friends. How many jars of preserves will each friend receive?

_____ jars

5. Mr. Gordan's art class needs 18 tubes of paint. The tubes come in packs of 3. How many packs does the class need?

_____ packs

6. Zoe draws a comic strip. The strip has 12 pictures. The pictures are arranged in 3 rows with the same number of pictures in each row. How many pictures are in each row?

_____ pictures in each row

Equal Groups with Remainders

CA Standards
KEY NS 3.2, KEY NS 3.0

When you divide, the number left over is called the remainder.
Use 7 objects to make 3 equal groups.
How many are in each group? How many are left over?

Step 1

Start with 7 objects.

Step 2

Make 3 equal groups until all the objects are used.

Step 3

There are 2 in each group. 1 object is left over.

$7 \div 3 = \underline{2}$ remainder 1

Number in all   Number of group   Number in each group   left over

Complete each division sentence.
Write the remainder.

Start with this many	Number of equal groups	Complete the division sentence
1. 13	2	_____ ÷ _____ = _____ remainder _____
2. 17	3	_____ ÷ _____ = _____ remainder _____
3. 23	4	_____ ÷ _____ = _____ remainder _____

Spiral Review (Chapter 21, Lesson 4) **KEY** NS 3.3, **KEY** NS 3.1

Write how many tens.
Multiply.

4.

_____ tens

$5 \times 10 = $ _____

Name _____ Date _____

Equal Groups with Remainders

CA Standards
KEY NS 3.2, **KEY** NS 3.0

1. 20 stickers are shared equally among 3 friends. How many does each friend get? How many are left over?

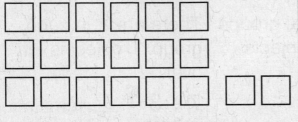

_____ stickers each
_____ left over

2. Megan has 18 pictures. She shares them equally among 4 of her friends. How many pictures does Megan have left over?

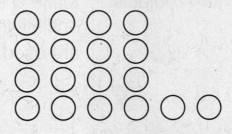

_____ pictures left over

3. Ruby, Anhil, Indira, and 2 other friends share 23 fruit snacks equally. How many fruit snacks does each friend receive? How many are left over?

Each has _____ fruit snacks.
There are _____ left over.

4. Jason picks 16 carrots. He ties them up into groups of 3. How many left over carrots does Jason have?

_____ left over

5. 24 beads are shared equally among 4 friends. How many beads did each friend receive? How many beads were left over?

Each friend received
_____ beads.
There are _____ beads left over.

6. Mr. Walsh has 28 cherries. He divides the cherries equally among 5 of his students, and keeps the rest for himself. How many cherries does he give to each student?

_____ cherries

Choose a Method

Darren bakes 20 cupcakes.
He gives an equal number of cupcakes to each of 4 friends.
How many cupcakes does each friend get?

What do you know?

- Darren bakes 20 cupcakes
- Gives cupcakes to 4 friends

Each friend gets _____ cupcakes.

Choose a method

- model equal groups
- use repeated subtraction
- write a number sentence

Choose a method. Solve.

Draw or write to explain.

1. June earns 18 reward stickers.
   She needs 6 to get a prize.
   How many prizes can June get?

   _____

2. David has 15 video games. He wants
   to put 3 video games in each box.
   How many boxes does he need?

   _____

3. Carmen has 21 marbles. She gives an
   equal number of marbles to each of
   3 friends. How many marbles did
   each friend receive?

   _____

 **Spiral Review** (Chapter 21, Lesson 5) **KEY** NS 3.0, **KEY** NS 3.3

4. There are 10 children in the book club. Each child
   gets 5 books. How many books are given to the book club?

   _____ books

Name _____ Date _____

Choose a Method

CA Standards
KEY NS 3.2, KEY NS 3.0

1. Sue gives 30 flower packets to her friends. Each friend gets 5 flower packets. How many friends does Sue give flower packets to?

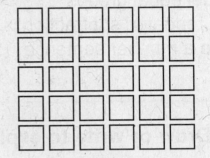

_____ friends

2. 3 friends share 8 toys equally. How many toys does each friend get? How many toys are left over?

Each friend gets _____ toys.

There are _____ toys left over.

3. There are 12 children playing tennis. There are 4 equal teams of children. How many children are on each team?

_____ children

4. 36 shells were collected by 4 children. Each child collected the same number of shells. How many shells did each child collect?

_____ shells

5. There are 20 bikes. The same number of bikes are in each of 4 racks. How many bikes are in each rack?

_____ bikes

6. Martin rents his skateboard to Alicia for 5 hours. Alicia pays the same amount for each hour. The total bill is $25. How much money does Martin get for each hour?

_____ per hour

Hands On: Count by 100s

CA Standards
KEY NS 1.1, NS 1.0

You can count up to one thousand by hundreds.

10 tens = one hundred   10 hundreds = one thousand

Draw the number with quick pictures. Write the number.

1. 2 hundreds

2. 4 hundreds

_____

_____

3. 5 hundreds

4. 3 hundreds

_____

_____

Spiral Review   (Chapter 22, Lesson 1) **KEY** NS 3.2, **KEY** NS 3.0

5. Draw dots to show the number in each group. Write how many are in each group.

$$15 \div 3 = \text{_____}$$

_____ in each group

Hands On: Count by 100s

CA Standards
KEY NS 1.1, NS 1.0

1. There are 100 flowers in each garden. Count to find the number of flowers in 7 gardens. How many flowers are in 7 gardens?

   100, 200, 300, _____, _____,

   _____, _____ flowers

2. Becca counted buttons using hundreds. Write the missing numbers she counted.

   100, 200, _____, _____, _____,

   600, 700, _____

3. There are 100 butterflies in each tree. How many butterflies are in 6 trees?

   _____, _____, _____, _____,

   _____, _____ butterflies

4. There are 482 people at the fair. Later, 100 more people come to the fair. How many people are at the fair now?

   _____ people

5. Liz modeled a number using 4 hundred flats. Jason took away 2 hundred flats and added 10 ten rods. What number is modeled now?

   _____

6. Ray modeled a number with 5 hundred flats. He took away 1 hundred flat and added 20 ten rods. What number is modeled now?

   _____

Hands On: Hundreds, Tens, Ones

CA Standards
KEY NS 1.1, NS 1.2

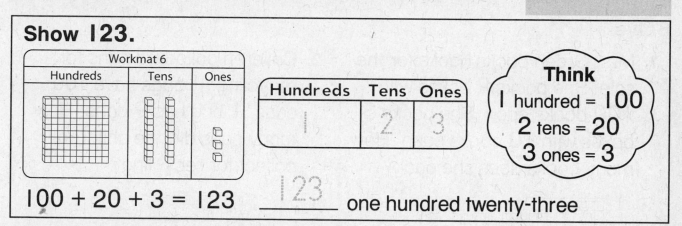

Show 123.

Workmat 6		
Hundreds	Tens	Ones

Hundreds	Tens	Ones
1	2	3

Think
1 hundred = 100
2 tens = 20
3 ones = 3

100 + 20 + 3 = 123   123 _____ one hundred twenty-three

Count hundreds, tens, and ones.
Write how many. Write the number.

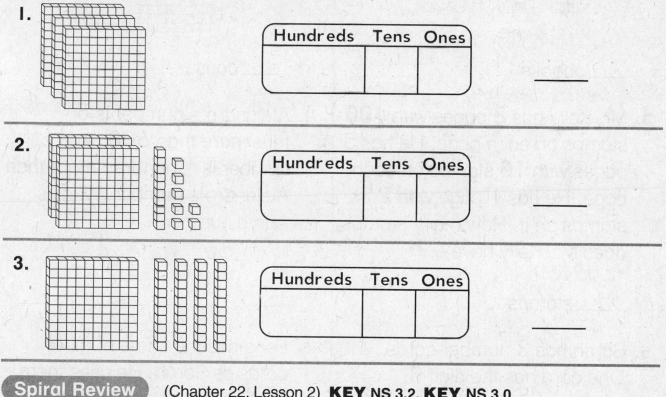

1.

Hundreds	Tens	Ones

_____

2.

Hundreds	Tens	Ones

_____

3.

Hundreds	Tens	Ones

_____

Spiral Review   (Chapter 22, Lesson 2) **KEY** NS 3.2, **KEY** NS 3.0

4. Divide and write the division sentence.

Start with this many.	Number in each group.	Divide. How many groups?
16	2	____ ÷ ____ = ____ groups

Name _____ Date _____

Hands On: Hundreds, Tens, Ones

Solve.

1. Mrs. Green packs books for the sale. She packs 2 boxes with 100 books each. She packs 3 boxes with 10 books each. How many books does she pack?

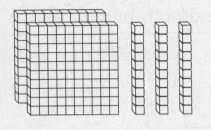

_____ books

2. Children collected cans for recycling. 4 bags have 100 cans. 1 bag has 9 cans. How many cans did the children collect for recycling?

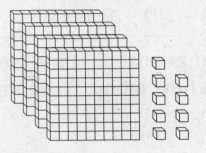

_____ cans

3. Mr. Kelly has 3 pages with 100 stamps on each page. He has 5 pages with 10 stamps on each page. He has 1 page with 2 stamps on it. How many stamps does Mr. Kelly have?

_____ stamps

4. Alejandro's number is 5 tens more than 600. Ann's number is 1 hundred more than Alejandro's number. What is Ann's number?

_____ _____

5. Sarah has 3 number cards. One card has the digit 8, another card has the digit 6, and the third card has the digit 0. If Sarah rearranges the order of the cards, what is the largest number she can make?

6. Feng has the same number cards as Sarah. He uses them to show a number that has 2 hundreds less that Sarah's and has no tens. What number did Feng show?

_____

Numbers Through 1,000

Show 921 in three different ways.

Way 1	Way 2	Way 3
Word form: Nine hundred twenty-one	Expanded form: $900 + 20 + 1$	Write hundreds, tens, and ones. (Place Value) 9 hundreds 2 tens 1 ones

Complete the table.

	Number	Word	Expanded Form	Place Value
1.	256	_____ _____	___ + ___ + ___	___ hundreds ___ tens ___ ones
2.	___	one hundred nineteen	___ + ___ + ___	___ hundreds ___ tens ___ ones
3.	___	_____ _____	$500 + 90 + 3$	___ hundreds ___ tens ___ ones

Spiral Review (Chapter 21, Lesson 3) **KEY** NS 3.3, **KEY** NS 3.1

```
◄———|———|———|———|———|———►
    0   5   10  15  20  25
```

Use the number line to divide.

4. $25 \div 5 =$ _____

5. $10 \div 5 =$ _____

Numbers Through 1,000

CA Standards
KEY NS 1.1, NS 1.2

1. Glen modeled a number with 6 hundred flats, 2 ten rods, and 5 one blocks. He takes away 1 hundred flat. What number does the model show now?

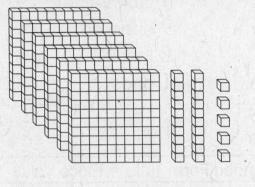

_____

2. Mia models the number 515. She then decides to model the number 545. What must she add to her model?

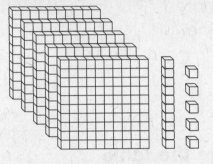

_____

3. Mona's number is 3 tens more than 500. Roy's number is 2 hundreds more than Mona's. Brian's number is 6 ones more than Roy's. What number do they each have?

Mona _____

Roy _____

Brian _____

4. Chris counts back by 100s. She counts 1,000, 900, 800, 700, 600. If she keeps counting in this fashion, what are the next two numbers she will say?

_____

5. Luis sells 215 tickets to the school concert. Carmen sells 200 tickets. How many tickets were sold in all?

_____ tickets

6. The school library received a donation of 600 books. The Parent Association donated 150 more books. How many books were donated to the library in all?

_____ books

Identify Place Value

CA Standards
KEY NS 1.1, NS 1.2

Find the value of the digits in 361.

Hundreds	Tens	Ones
3	6	1

To find the value of a digit, find the value of its place.

$$300 + 60 + 1 \_\_\_\_\_$$

Write the number.

1. $400 + 20 + 5$ _____

2. $2 + 40 + 500$ _____

3. $200 + 70 + 1$ _____

4. $300 + 10 + 2$ _____

5. $6 + 30 + 100$ _____

6. $700 + 40 + 6$ _____

Circle the value of the underlined digit.

7. 52<u>8</u>

    800   80   8

8. 6<u>5</u>1

    500   50   5

9. <u>7</u>65

    700   70   7

10. 38<u>4</u>

    400   40   4

Spiral Review (Chapter 22, Lesson 4) KEY NS 3.2, KEY NS 3.0

Complete each division sentence. Write the remainder.

	Number	Divisor	Division Sentence
11.	7	3	___ ÷ ___ = ___ remainder ___
12.	15	6	___ ÷ ___ = ___ remainder ___

Use with text pp. 457–458

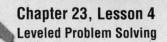
Identify Place Value

CA Standards
KEY NS 1.1, NS 1.2

1. Mr. Vargas helps to make 632 sandwiches for the fair. What is the value of the digit 6 in 632?

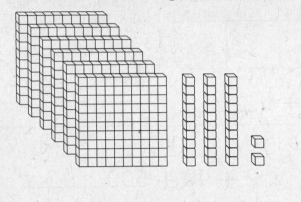

_____

2. Nina has 200 + 40 + 9 glitter stickers. How many glitter stickers does Nina have?

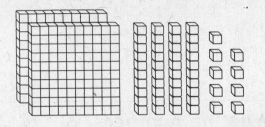

_____ glitter stickers

3. David has 871 stamps in his stamp collection. What is the value of the digit 7 in 871?

_____

4. Claire has 300 trading cards in a red box. She has 50 trading cards in a blue box. She has 4 trading cards in a green box. How many cards does Claire have?

_____ trading cards

5. On Friday 795 people visited the amusement park. On Saturday 200 more people visited the amusement park. On Sunday 55 fewer people visited than on Saturday. How many people visited the amusement park on Sunday?

_____

6. Parker's school printed 800 tickets for the talent show. They sold 600 tickets the week before the show, 80 tickets the day before the show, and 9 tickets an hour before the show. How many tickets did they sell in all?

_____ tickets

Make a Table

CA Standards
SDAP 2.1, SDAP 2.2

Sometimes you can make a table to help solve a problem.

The coach orders 4 sheet pizzas for a team party.
Each sheet pizza has 20 slices.
How many slices are in 4 pizzas?

Solve. Make a table.
Count slices for 4 pizzas.

Pizzas	1	2	3	4
Slices	20	40	60	80

There are ___80___ slices in 4 pizzas.

Solve. Make a table.

1. Each pack of water has
   6 bottles. How many bottles
   are in 4 packs?

Packs	1			
Bottles	6			

_____ bottles

2. There are 10 apples in each
   bag. How many apples are
   in 3 bags?

Bags	1			
Apples	10			

_____ apples

Spiral Review   (Chapter 22, Lesson 5) **KEY** NS 3.2, **KEY** NS 3.0

Choose a method. Solve.

3. Steven has 6 boxes.
   He puts 5 books in each
   box. How many books does
   Steven have?

_____ books

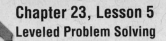
Make a Table

CA Standards
SDAP 2.2, SDAP 2.1

1. Children in soccer camp do 20 practice kicks each day. The camp lasts for 5 days. How many kicks do the children do by the end of camp?

Days	Kicks
1	20
2	40
3	
4	
5	

_____ kicks

2. There are 48 donuts waiting to be boxed. Each box holds 12 donuts. How many boxes are needed to box the donuts?

Box	1	2		
Donuts	12	24		

_____ boxes

3. Rachel's family went on a road trip. They drove for 7 days. Each day they drove 100 miles. How far did they drive?

_____ miles

4. Victor reads 20 pages every day. The book he is reading is 120 pages long. How long will it take Victor to read his book?

_____ days

5. Sacha embroiders 3 roses on patches for a quilt. Her design has roses on every other patch. If her quilt is made up of 100 patches, how many roses will Sacha have to embroider?

_____ roses

6. How many patches on Sacha's quilt will not have roses embroidered on them?

_____ patches

Name _____ Date _____

Regroup Tens as Hundreds

CA Standards
KEY NS 1.3, NS 1.0

You can regroup 10 tens as 1 hundred.

Show 234 in two ways.

1 hundred 13 tens 4 ones

Hundreds	Tens	Ones

Regroup 10 tens as 1 hundred

2 hundreds 3 tens 4 ones

Hundreds	Tens	Ones

Complete the chart.

	Number	Regroup 10 tens as 1 hundred
1.	6 hundreds 14 tens 9 ones	____ hundreds ____ tens ____ ones
2.	8 hundreds 11 tens 4 ones	____ hundreds ____ tens ____ ones
3.	2 hundreds 12 tens 1 ones	____ hundreds ____ tens ____ ones
4.	1 hundreds 17 tens 2 ones	____ hundreds ____ tens ____ ones
5.	5 hundreds 13 tens 7 ones	____ hundreds ____ tens ____ ones
6.	3 hundreds 19 tens 0 ones	____ hundreds ____ tens ____ ones
7.	7 hundreds 16 tens 5 ones	____ hundreds ____ tens ____ ones
8.	4 hundreds 13 tens 3 ones	____ hundreds ____ tens ____ ones

Spiral Review (Chapter 23, Lesson 01) **KEY** NS 1.1, NS1.0

9. Draw the number with quick pictures. Write the number.

4 hundreds

____

Regroup Tens as Hundreds

CA Standards
KEY NS 1.1, MR 1.0

You can draw a picture to help you solve problems about hundreds, tens, and ones.

Draw or write to explain.

1. Mrs. Green packs books for the sale. She packs 2 boxes with 100 books. She packs 3 boxes with 10 books.

   How many books does she pack?

   _____ books

2. Children collected cans for recycling. 4 bags have 100 cans. 1 bag has 9 cans.

   How many cans did the children collect for recycling?

   _____ cans

3. Mr. Kelly has 3 pages with 100 stamps on each page. He has 5 pages with 10 stamps on each page. He has 1 page with 2 stamps on it. How many stamps does Mr. Kelly have?

   _____ stamps

4. Rosa packed 5 cartons of 10 dishes and 3 cartons of 10 mugs. How many items did Rosa pack?

   _____

5. Michael has 75 hotdogs that he wants to pack in cases of ten. How many full cases will Michael have?

   _____

6. Joseph has 6 cases of 50 muffins. He wants to transfer them to the larger 100 case. How many 100 cases will he need?

   _____

Name _____ Date _____

Compare Three-Digit Numbers

CA Standards
KEY NS 1.3, NS 1.1

Use place value to compare and order numbers.

Compare the hundreds.	Compare the tens.	Compare the ones.
3̲23 2̲20 3̲26	3 2̲ 3 3 2̲ 6	32 3̲ 32 6̲
220 is less than 323 and 326.	323 and 326 both have 2 tens.	323 is less than 326.

So, ___220___ is least.

least, ⟶ ___220___, ___323___, ___326___, ⟵ greatest

Compare the numbers.

Write >, <, or = in the ◯ .

1. 525 ◯ 520

2. 212 ◯ 221

3. 144 ◯ 200

4. 763 ◯ 763

5. 838 ◯ 837

6. 626 ◯ 719

7. 295 ◯ 297

8. 410 ◯ 401

9. 355 ◯ 365

Spiral Review   (Chapter 23, Lesson 2) **KEY** NS 1.1, NS 1.2

Write how many. Then write the number.

Number	Write how many hundreds, tens, and ones.			Write the number
	Hundreds	Tens	Ones	
10.				_____
11.				_____

Use with text pp. 471–472

Compare Three-Digit Numbers

CA Standards
KEY NS 1.1, KEY NS 1.3

The table shows how many miles it is to Chicago from other cities. Use the table for problems 1–4.

How Many Miles to Chicago	
City	Miles
Atlanta	674
Buffalo	538
Boston	963
Lexington	377
Baltimore	701

1. Don travels from Atlanta to Chicago. Bill travels from Baltimore to Chicago. Who travels farther?

_____

2. Troy drives from Buffalo to Chicago. Leng drives from Lexington to Chicago. Who drives farther?

_____

3. Mrs. Davis drives from Baltimore to Chicago. Mrs. Logan drives to Chicago from a city that is 27 miles closer. Which city does Mrs. Logan drive from?

_____

4. Susan made a 754 mile round trip from her city to Chicago and back. Which city did she drive from?

_____

5. John traveled 325 miles on vacation. Eric traveled 875 miles on vacation. Matt traveled 850 miles on vacation. Who traveled the most miles on vacation?

_____

6. Cindy's family drove 525 miles. Elizabeth's family drove 555 miles. How much farther did Elizabeth's family drive than Cindy's?

_____ miles

Before, After, and Between

CA Standards
KEY NS 1.3, MR 1.2

A number line can help you find a number that is just before, just after, or between other numbers.

← 210 211 212 213 214 215 216 217 218 219 220 221 222 223 224 225 →

210 is just before 211.

220 is between 219 and 221.

225 is just after 224.

Write the number.

	Before	Between	After
1.	_____, 650	646, _____, 648	652, _____
2.	_____, 649	650, _____, 652	653, _____
3.	_____, 653	654, _____, 656	657, _____
4.	_____, 642	643, _____, 645	646, _____
5.	_____, 655	640, _____, 642	651, _____
6.	_____, 646	652, _____, 654	647, _____

Spiral Review (Chapter 23, Lesson 3) **KEY** NS 1.1, NS 1.2

Complete the number.

	Number	Word Form	Expanded Form	Place Value
7.	735		_____ + _____ + _____	_____ hundreds _____ tens _____ ones
8.	_____	two hundred seventy-four	_____ + _____ + _____	_____ hundreds _____ tens _____ ones

Name _____ Date _____

Hands On: Before, After, and Between

Draw a picture or a number line on a separate sheet of paper to help you solve the problems.

Draw or write to explain.

1. Anita has tickets numbered from 348 to 353. She uses one of the tickets.

←—+——+——+——+——+——+——+——+——+——+——+——→
345 346 347 348 349 350 351 352 353 354 355

She has numbers 348, 349, 351, 352, and 353. Which ticket does she use?

ticket _____

2. Jon writes missing numbers on a number line. The number between 579 and 581 is missing. What number does Jon write?

←—+——+——+——+——+——+——+——+——+——+——+——→
575 576 577 578 579 ___ 581 582 583 584 585

_____

3. Mr. Ling buys three movie tickets. The tickets are sold in order from least to greatest. The first ticket sold today is number 411. What are the next two ticket numbers?

_____ and _____

4. Ann read three pages in a book. The last page she read was page number 113. What are the other two pages that Ann read?

_____ and _____

5. Serena thinks of a number. The number she counts is between 113 and 117. The number comes just before a number that you say when you count by 4s. What is the number?

_____

6. Gus thinks of a number that is between 518 and 522. The number has 1 ten. What number is Gus thinking of?

_____

Order Three-Digit Numbers

Use place value to order numbers.
Order the numbers from least to greatest.

| 334 | 441 | 330 |

Compare the hundreds. 441 is the greatest.
Compare the tens. Both 334 and 330 have 3 tens.
Compare the ones. 330 < 334.

Write the numbers in order from least to greatest.

1. 235, 352, 225   _____ < _____ < _____

2. 652, 781, 358   _____ < _____ < _____

Write the numbers in order from greatest to least.

3. 713, 476, 798   _____ > _____ > _____

4. 469, 356, 785   _____ > _____ > _____

Spiral Review (Chapter 23, Lesson 4) **KEY** NS 1.1, NS 1.2

Write the number.

5. 200 + 40 + 9 = _____

6. 100 + 60 + 2 = _____

Order Three-Digit Numbers

CA Standards
KEY NS 1.1, NS 1.3

The table shows how many miles it is to Chicago from other cities. Use the table for problems 1–2.

How Many Miles to Chicago	
City	Miles
Atlanta	674
Buffalo	538
Boston	963
Lexington	377
Baltimore	701

1. List the names of the cities in order from greatest distance to least distance from Chicago.

_____

_____

2. List the cities distance from Chicago in order from least to greatest.

_____

_____

Order the numbers to solve.

3. License plates have the numbers 318, 813, 138, 381, and 183. What are the license plate numbers in order from least to greatest?

_____

4. Corbin has cards numbered 260, 206, 602, 620, and 226. He puts the cards in order from greatest to least. How does Corbin order the cards?

_____

5. Use the digits 4, 5, and 6 to write as many three-digit numbers as you can, using each digit only once. Then write the numbers from least to greatest.

_____

6. Gretchen sold 615 raffle tickets, Mark sold 650, Ira sold 655, and Kemal sold 625. Write the names of the children in order from who sold the most to who sold the least.

_____

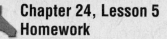
Count Dollars and Cents

CA Standards
KEY NS 5.1, **KEY** NS 5.2

Use a dollar sign and a decimal point to show money.

one dollar bill $1.00   five-dollar bill $5.00   ten dollar bill $10.00

Count and write the total value of the bills and coins.

1. $ _____

2. $ _____

3. $ _____

Draw bills and coins to show the amount.

4. $8.75

5. 16 dollars and twenty-nine cents

Spiral Review   (Chapter 23, Lesson 5) **SDAP 2.1, SDAP 2.2**

Solve by making a table.

6. Joshua jogs 3 miles each day.

He jogs the same distance every day for 7 days.

How far has Joshua jogged after 7 days?   _____ miles

Name _____ Date _____

Count Dollars and Cents

CA Standards
KEY NS 5.1, KEY NS 5.2

1. Dora has 3 dollars 2 quarters and 1 dime. How much money does she have?

_____

2. Ben has one five dollar bill, 2 one dollar bills and 3 quarters. How much money does he have?

_____

3. Rachel collected 6 quarters and 7 dimes. How much money did she collect?

_____

4. Miguel collected $3.00 more than Rachel. How much money did he collect?

_____

5. Linda needs $1.25 in exact change to ride the bus. She has only quarters. How many quarters must Linda use to ride the bus?

_____

6. Ben has $1.00 in coins. He has 7 coins. Five of his coins are dimes. What are the other two coins?

_____

Comparison Problems

CA Standard
AF 1.3

The table shows the distance of each hiking trail. How much longer is the Wandering Lake Trail than the Roaming Pine Trail?

Eagle Mountain Hiking Trails	
Trail	**Distance**
Whispering Leaves Trail	5 miles
Roaming Pine Trail	7 miles
River Walk Trail	14 miles
Wandering Lake Trail	18 miles

What do you know?   Roaming Pine Trail is 7 miles long.
Wandering Lake Trail is 18 miles long.

Choose the operation: I need to subtract.

Write the parts you know: Wandering Lake Trail ___18 miles___ is greater

than Roaming Pine Trail ___7 miles___

Write a number sentence: ___18 miles___ − ___7 miles___ = ___11 miles___

Solve.

1. Morgan's family hikes two of the Eagle mountain trails. They hike a total of 19 miles. One of the trails hiked was the River Walk Trail. What was the other trail?

_____

Spiral Review **(Chapter 23, Lesson 5)** SDAP 2.1, SDAP 2.2

Solve. Complete the table.

Brownies	12			
Baking sheet	1	2	3	4

2. A few children baked brownies.
   They baked 12 brownies on each baking sheet.
   How many brownies were baked on 4 baking sheets? _____

Name _____ Date _____

Comparison Problems

School Supplies	Price
Composition Book	$0.95
Pack of Pens	$1.25
Sharpener	$0.25
Back Pack	$3.00

Solve using the table above.

1. How much more does the pack of pens cost than the composition book?

   $1.25 − $0.95 = _____

2. How much more does the pack of pens cost than the sharpener?

   $1.25 − $0.25 = _____

3. Karen bought a back pack and another item. The other item cost $2.05 less than the back pack. What is the other item Karen bought?

   _____

4. James bought a composition book. How much more does the composition book cost than a sharpener?

   _____

5. Gloria buys a pack of pens and a sharpener. She then buys another item that costs two times as much as the pens and sharpener. What other item did Gloria buy?

   _____

6. Tyrone has $4.00. He wants to buy a back pack and a composition book. Does he have enough money?

   _____

Hands On: Add Hundreds

CA Standards
KEY NS 2.2, MR 1.2

The fact $1 + 4 = 5$ can help you add $100 + 400$.

1 hundreds	100
+ 4 hundreds	+ 400
5 hundreds	500

Use the basic fact to help you add hundreds.

1. $5 + 2 =$ _____

    5 hundreds + 2 hundreds = _____ hundreds

    $500 + 200 =$ _____

2. $3 + 6 =$ _____

    3 hundreds + 6 hundreds = _____ hundreds

    $300 + 600 =$ _____

3.
4	4 hundreds	400
+ 5	+ 5 hundreds	+ 500
	hundreds	

4.
2	2 hundreds	200
+ 4	+ 4 hundreds	+ 400
	hundreds	

Spiral Review (Chapter 24, Lesson 1) **KEY** NS 1.1, NS 1.0

Regroup. Fill in the blanks.

5. 2 hundreds 14 tens 5 ones

    _____ hundreds   _____ tens   _____ ones

6. 6 hundreds 11 tens 8 ones

    _____ hundreds   _____ tens   _____ ones

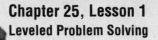
Hands On: Add Hundreds

CA Standards
KEY NS 2.2, MR 1.2

Use the basic fact to help you add hundreds.
Draw or write to explain.

1. There were 300 children who saw the movie. There were 100 adults who saw the movie. How many people saw the movie altogether?

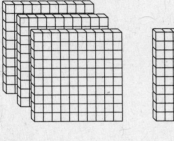

_____ people

2. There are 200 girls and 200 boys eating lunch. How many children are eating lunch altogether?

_____ children

3. There were 500 children at the concert on Saturday. There were 300 children at the concert on Sunday. How many children attended the concert in all?

_____ children

4. There are 400 beads in a large package. There are 200 beads in a small package. How many beads are in both packages?

_____ beads

5. Jewel has 700 stickers in her old sticker book. She has 200 more stickers in her new sticker book. How many stickers does Jewel have altogether?

_____ stickers

6. Michael collected 100 action figures. Jill collected three times as many action figures as Michael. How many action figures do Michael and Jill have altogether?

_____ action figures

Hands On: Regroup Ones

CA Standards
KEY NS 2.2, MR 1.2

Find 318 and 125.

H	T	O
3	1	8
+ 1	2	5
4	4	3

First add the ones. Regroup 10 ones as 1 ten. Next add the tens. Then add the hundreds.

Add.

1. 434
    + 248

2. 149
    + 323

3. 550
    + 436

4. 721
    + 159

5. 262
    + 27

6. 345
    + 202

7. 643
    +   8

8. 172
    + 114

Spiral Review (Chapter 24, Lesson 2) **KEY** NS 1.3, **KEY** NS 1.1

Compare the numbers.

Write >, <, or =.

9. 417 _____ 417

10. 325 _____ 330

11. 555 _____ 575

12. 615 _____ 605

Use with text pp. 497–498

Hands On: Regroup Ones

CA Standards
KEY NS 2.2, MR 1.2

**Use models, draw a picture, or write to help you
solve problems with regrouping.**

1. A package has 362 red lettuce
   seeds. Another package has
   419 green lettuce seeds.
   How many seeds are in both
   packages?

   _____ seeds

2. Sammy has a box with 156
   large buttons. He has a
   box with 227 small buttons.
   How many buttons does he
   have in all?

   _____ buttons

3. There are 286 first graders who
   play soccer. There are 309
   second graders who play soccer.
   How many children play soccer
   altogether?

   _____ children

4. Mrs. Santos drives 135 miles
   on Monday. She drives
   109 miles on Tuesday. How
   many miles does she drive
   in all?

   _____ miles

5. Luke's team scored 346
   points. They beat Kyle's team
   by 20 points. What was the
   total number of points scored in
   the game?

   _____ points

6. 145 children are members of
   the Nature club this year. There
   are 10 more children in the
   Chess club than in the Nature
   club. How many children are in
   the Chess or Nature club?

   _____ children

Hands On: Regroup Tens

CA Standards
KEY NS 2.2, MR 1.2

Find **263 + 474.**

H	T	O
2	6	3
+ 4	7	4
7	3	7

First add the ones.
Regroup 10 tens as 1 hundred.
Next add the tens.
Then add the hundreds.

Add.

1. 152
   + 181

2. 590
   + 238

3. 627
   + 92

4. 372
   + 165

5. 486
   + 40

6. 741
   + 198

7. 168
   + 250

8. 284
   + 234

Spiral Review (Chapter 24, Lesson 3) **KEY** NS 1.3

Write the number.

Before	Between	After
9. _____, 156	158, _____, 160	318, _____
10. _____, 197	205, _____, 207	222, _____

Use with text pp. 499–500

Hands On: Regroup Tens

CA Standards
KEY NS 2.2, MR 1.2

You can use models or draw a picture
to help you solve problems.

1. There were 382 people at
the ballpark before the game
started. Another 174 people
arrived after the game started.
How many people in all were at
the ballpark?

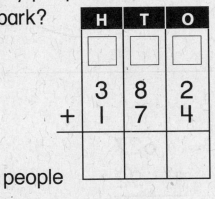

_____ people

2. Lyle has 243 stamps from
Canada. He has 195 stamps
from Mexico. How many
stamps does Lyle have in all?

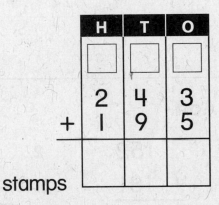

_____ stamps

3. The library has 292 books
about sea animals. It has
541 books about land animals.
How many books about animals
does the library have
altogether?

_____ books

4. Max's family drives 275 miles
to visit her grandmother. Then
they drive 52 miles to visit her
uncle. How many miles does
mail's family drive in all?

_____ miles

5. The boys score 145 points in a
game. The girls score 20 points
more than the boys. How many
points do the players score
altogether?

_____ points

6. The Eagles hockey team has
two times as many fans as the
Sharks team. The Sharks have
153 fans. How many fans do
the Eagles have?

_____ fans

Practice Adding Three-Digit Numbers

CA Standards
KEY NS 2.2, NS 2.0

When you add three-digit numbers decide whether you need to regroup.

Find $300 + 400$

$$\begin{array}{r} 300 \\ + 400 \\ \hline \end{array}$$ mental math

Find $774 + 17$

$$\begin{array}{r} 774 \\ + 17 \\ \hline \end{array}$$ Regroup tens

Find $482 + 37$

$$\begin{array}{r} 482 \\ + 37 \\ \hline \end{array}$$ Regroup hundreds

Add. Decide whether you need to regroup.

1. $\begin{array}{r} 542 \\ + 65 \\ \hline \end{array}$

2. $\begin{array}{r} 384 \\ + 445 \\ \hline \end{array}$

3. $\begin{array}{r} 200 \\ + 300 \\ \hline \end{array}$

4. $\begin{array}{r} 576 \\ + 93 \\ \hline \end{array}$

5. $\begin{array}{r} 908 \\ + 48 \\ \hline \end{array}$

6. $\begin{array}{r} 675 \\ + 108 \\ \hline \end{array}$

7. $\begin{array}{r} 237 \\ + 153 \\ \hline \end{array}$

8. $\begin{array}{r} 226 \\ + 233 \\ \hline \end{array}$

9. $\begin{array}{r} 240 \\ + 213 \\ \hline \end{array}$

10. $\begin{array}{r} 300 \\ + 600 \\ \hline \end{array}$

11. $\begin{array}{r} 123 \\ + 12 \\ \hline \end{array}$

12. $\begin{array}{r} 355 \\ + 36 \\ \hline \end{array}$

Spiral Review (Chapter 24, Lesson 4) **KEY** NS 1.3, **KEY** NS 1.1

Write the numbers in order from greatest to least.

13. $565, 545, 490, 525$ _____ > _____ > _____ > _____

Use with text pp. 501–502

Practice Adding Three-Digit Numbers

CA Standards
KEY NS 2.2, NS 2.0

1. Angel reads two books about soccer. One book has 135 pages. The other book has 145 pages. How many pages does Angel read in all?

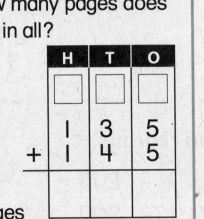

H	T	O
☐	☐	☐
1	3	5
+ 1	4	5

_____ pages

2. A printer prints 500 posters on Saturday and 300 posters on Sunday. How many posters were printed over the weekend?

5 + 3 _____

_____ posters

3. Jesse places 250 photographs in one album and 150 photographs in another. How many photographs did Jesse place in the albums?

_____ photographs

4. Brenda collected 315 shells over the summer. Her sister collected 290 shells. How many shells did they collect in all?

_____ shells

5. There were 145 fans at Monday night's game. 85 more fans attended Tuesday night's game than Monday's game. How many fans attended Monday's and Tuesday's games?

_____ fans

6. There were 100 athletes at the track competition. Each athlete brought 2 guests. How many guests and athletes attended the track competition?

_____ guests and athletes

Multi-Step Problems

On Saturday the Morgan family drives 150 miles on vacation. On Sunday they drive 75 more miles than they did on Saturday. How many miles did they drive both days in all?

What do you need to find out?

| How many miles were driven on Sunday? | How many miles were driven in all? |

Solve.

How many miles were driven on Sunday?

How many miles were driven in all?

150 ⊕ 75 = 225 miles   150 ⊕ 225 = 375 miles

Solve. Draw or write to explain.

1. Gia and Rob each read 25 pages each night.
   Gia reads for 5 nights. Rob reads for 3 nights.
   How many pages do they read in all?

   _____ pages

2. Kevin wins 125 points at the arcade. Then he wins 70 more points. Allison wins 200 points at the arcade. Who wins the most points?

   _____

Spiral Review (Chapter 24, Lesson 5) **KEY** NS 5.1, **KEY** NS 5.2

Count and write the total value of the bills and coins.

  $ _____

Multi-Step Problems

CA Standards
KEY NS 2.2, NS 2.0

Solve. Show your work.

1. Emma sewed 20 buttons on each puppet. Rachel sewed 10 buttons on each puppet. They made 5 puppets together. How many buttons did they sew in all?

Rachel:

____ + ____ + ____ + ____

+ ____ = ____

Emma:

____ + ____ + ____ + ____ +

____ = ____

_____ buttons in all

2. Alejandro has 3 cases of comics. Justin has 5 cases of comics. If Alejandro has 50 comics in each case and Justin has 20 comics in each case who has the most comics?

Alejandro:

____ + ____ + ____ = ____

Justin:

____ + ____ + ____ + ____

+ ____ = ____ comics

_____

3. Last year the Hiking Club hiked 110 miles. This year they hiked two times as many miles. How many miles did they hike in the last two years?

_____ miles

4. Rodney saves 25 coins each week. Justin saves 30 coins each week. How many coins will Rodney and Justin have in all after 4 weeks?

_____ coins

5. Todd's score is 225. Anna's score is 150 points more than Todd's. Alan's score is 50 points more than Anna's. What is Alan's score?

_____ points

6. What is the total of Todd's score and Alan's score?

_____ points

Hands On: Subtract Hundreds

CA Standard
KEY NS 2.2, MR 1.2

The fact $8 - 6 = 2$ can help you subtract $800 - 600$.

8	8 hundreds	800
-6	-6 hundreds	-600
2	2 hundreds	200

Use the subtraction fact to help you subtract hundreds.

1. $5 - 3 =$ _____

   5 hundreds $-$ 3 hundreds = _____ hundreds

   $500 - 300 =$ _____

2. $7 - 4 =$ _____

   7 hundreds $-$ 4 hundreds = _____ hundreds

   $700 - 400 =$ _____

3.
9	9 hundreds	900
-5	-5 hundreds	-500
	hundreds	

4.
6	6 hundreds	600
-2	-2 hundreds	-200
	hundreds	

5.
8	8 hundreds	800
-3	-3 hundreds	-300
	hundreds	

6.
7	7 hundreds	700
-1	-1 hundreds	-100
	hundreds	

Spiral Review (Chapter 25, Lesson 1) **KEY** NS 2.2, MR 1.2

Add.

7. $300 + 500 =$ _____

8. $200 + 300 =$ _____

Hands On: Subtract Hundreds

CA Standards
KEY NS 2.2, MR 1.2

Solve.

1. The bookstore sells 400 Story books and 500 nature books. How many more nature books than story books does the bookstore sell?

_____ nature books

2. There are 700 adults and 200 childern at a concert. How many more adults than childern are at the concert?

$700 - 200 =$ _____ adults

3. A pilot flies 700 miles on Monday. She flies 900 miles on Wednesday. How many more miles does she fly on Wednesday than on Monday?

_____ miles

4. Lisa delivers 200 newspapers on weekdays. She delivers 400 newspapers on weekends. How many more newspapers does she deliver on weekends than on weekdays?

_____ newspapers

5. Lisa collected 500 stickers. Jackson collected 200 fewer stickers than Lisa. How many stickers does Jackson have?

_____ Stickers

6. Lance and Robin both volunteer on weekends. Lance volunteered 200 hours last year. Robin volunteered 100 hours. How many more hours did Lance volunteer than Robin?

_____ hours

Name _____ Date _____

Hands On: Regroup Tens

CA Standards
KEY NS 2.2, MR 1.2

Find 362 − 148.

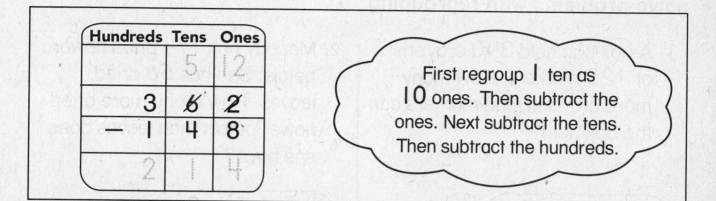

Hundreds	Tens	Ones
3	5̸6	1̸2
− 1	4	8
2	1	4

First regroup 1 ten as 10 ones. Then subtract the ones. Next subtract the tens. Then subtract the hundreds.

Subtract.

1.

Hundreds	Tens	Ones
2	3̸	5̸
− 1	1	7

2.

Hundreds	Tens	Ones
3	8̸	4̸
−		8

3.

Hundreds	Tens	Ones
5	9̸	3̸
− 2	6	5

4.

Hundreds	Tens	Ones
4	6̸	7̸
−	4	6

5.

Hundreds	Tens	Ones
8	2	8
− 1	1	2

6.

Hundreds	Tens	Ones
7	4̸	6̸
− 2	1	9

Spiral Review (Chapter 25, Lesson 2) **KEY** NS 2.2, MR 1.2

Add.

7.
```
  403
+ 238
```

8.
```
  568
+ 219
```

9.
```
  729
+  16
```

Hands On: Regroup Tens

CA Standards
KEY NS 2.2, MR 1.2

You can use models or draw a picture to help you solve problems with regrouping.

1. A box can hold 340 crayons or 125 markers. How many more crayons than markers can the box hold?

Hundreds	Tens	Ones
3	4	0
− 1	2	5

_____ crayons

2. Monday has 174 dried flower petals. She has 56 dried leaves. How many more dried flower petals than leaves does she have?

Hundreds	Tens	Ones
1	7	4
−	5	6

_____ flower petals

3. Ms. Lee's class collects 562 cans of food. Mr. Ramsey's class collects 247 cans. How many more cans does Ms. Lee's class collect than Mr. Ramsey's class?

_____ cans

4. The distance from River City to Old Town is 384 miles. Mr. Lang drives 258 miles. How many more miles does he need to drive?

_____ miles

5. There are 355 girls at Ellis elementary school. There are 292 boys. How many more girls attend the school than boys?

_____ girls

6. Joseph swims the 400 meter race. So far he has swum 120 meters. How much further does Joseph have to swim?

_____ meters

Hands On: Regroup Hundreds

Find 448 − 265.

Hundreds	Tens	Ones
3	14	
4̶	4̶	8
− 2	6	5
1	8	3

First subtract the ones. Regroup 1 hundred as 10 tens. Next subtract the tens. Then subtract the hundreds.

Subtract.

1. 633
   −442

2. 465
   −182

3. 747
   −273

4. 928
   −397

5. 328
   −144

6. 236
   −151

7. 557
   −296

8. 327
   −45

9. 468
   −297

10. 526
   −293

11. 654
   −392

12. 818
   −626

Spiral Review   (Chapter 25, Lesson 3) **KEY** NS 2.2, MR 1.2

Add.

13. 345
   +183

14. 676
   +242

15. 729
   +16

Hands On: Regroup Hundreds

You can use models or draw a picture to help you solve problems.

1. Leo's team scores 109 points in their first game. They score 87 points in their second game. How many more points do they score in their first game?

Hundreds	Tens	Ones
X̶	Ø	9
−	8	7

_____ points

2. Jake has 637 coins from Asia. He has 253 coins from South America. How many more coins does Jake have from Asia than from South America?

Hundreds	Tens	Ones
6	3	7
− 2	5	3

_____ coins

3. The snack bar had 228 customers on Monday and 193 customers on Tuesday. How many more customers did the snack bar have on Monday?

_____ customers

4. Pedro's class collects 740 cans to recycle. Bella's class collects 916 cans to recycle. How many more cans does Bella's class collect than Pedro's class?

_____ cans

5. Calvin has 345 coins in his jar. Jerry has 192 fewer coins in his jar. How many coins does Jerry have?

_____ coins

6. Mrs. James drove 456 miles on vacation. Mr. James drove 472 miles to meet her. How much further did Mr. James drive than Mrs. James?

_____ miles

Practice Subtracting Three-Digit Numbers

When you subtract three-digit numbers, decide whether you need to regroup.

Find 600 − 400	Find 567 − 59	Find 667 − 86
600	567	667
−400 mental math.	−59 Regroup tens.	−86 Regroup hundreds.

Subtract. Decide whether you need to regroup.

1. 516
   − 23

2. 307
   −153

3. 425
   −312

4. 519
   −194

5. 122
   −22

6. 265
   −107

7. 600
   −200

8. 744
   −136

Spiral Review (Chapter 25, Lesson 4) **KEY** NS 2.2, NS 2.0

Add. Decide whether you need to regroup.

9. 345
   +183

10. 676
   +242

11. 729
   +16

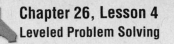
Practice Subtracting 3-Digit Numbers

CA Standard
KEY NS 2.2

Use the supply list to solve.

Toy Shop Gifts	
Items	**Number in stock**
Panda bear key chain	386
Giraffe ruler	459
Lion mask	678
Penguin puppet	495
Polar bear poster	149

1. How many more panda bear key chains are there than polar bear posters?

   _____

2. Margo buys 54 polar bear posters. How many more polar bear posters are left?

   _____

3. How many more penguin puppets are there than giraffe rulers?

   _____

4. 290 lion masks are sold. How many lion masks are left in stock?

   _____ lion masks

5. The gift store returns 90 panda bear key chains to the manufacturer. How many more panda bear key chains are there now than polar bear posters?

   _____ panda bear key chains

6. The gift shop sold some penguin puppets. There are now the same number of penguin puppets as polar bear posters. How many penguin puppets were sold?

   _____ penguin puppets

Write a Number Sentence

**The second grade went to the Science Museum.
They spent 40 minutes at the space show.
Then they went to the exhibits for 90 minutes.**

Add when you need to find how many there are in all.
How many minutes did the second grade
spend at the museum altogether?

__40__ $\oplus$ __90__ = __130__ minutes

Subtract when you need to find how many more.
How many more minutes did they spend
at the exhibits than at the show?

__90__ $\ominus$ __40__ = __50__ minutes

Choose the operation. Solve.

1. The bus took 65 minutes to get to the museum and 40 minutes to
   return to school. How many minutes was the class on the bus?

   65 ◯ 40 = _____ minutes

2. This year 140 second graders went on the trip. Last year
   159 children took the trip. How many more children went
   on the trip last year?

   159 ◯ 140 = _____ children

Spiral Review (Chapter 25, Lesson 5) **KEY NS 2.2, NS 2.0**

Solve.

3. Sandra collects 20 cans each day for recycling.
   Sharon collects 15 cans each day. After 5 days
   how many cans have they collected altogether? _____

Write a Number Sentence

CA Standard
KEY NS 2.2, MR 2.0

1. Joseph must stock the grocery store shelves with 177 cans of soup. He has already stacked 96 cans. How many more cans does Joseph need to stack?

Hundreds	Tens	Ones
X	7	7
−	9	6

_____ more cans

2. At the end of the day there were 92 boxes of cereal left. There were 389 boxes at the beginning of the day. How many boxes were sold?

Hundreds	Tens	Ones
3	8	9
−	9	2

_____ boxes of cereal

3. 256 students at Central Elementary School take music lessons. 112 of them play more than one instrument. How many students play one instrument?

_____ students

4. Vincent trains for 155 minutes each day. So far today he has trained for 85 minutes. How much longer does he need to train?

_____ minutes

5. Mischa's class bought 350 T-shirts to sell as a fund raiser. They sold 150 T-shirts on Monday. On Tuesday, they sold 50 fewer T-shirts than they did on Monday. How many T-shirts do they have left?

_____ T-shirts

6. Mr. Phillip wants to sell 200 more books this month than he did last month. Last month he sold 432 books. This month he sold 591 books. Write a number sentence to show whether Mr. Phillip reached his goal.

_____

Hands On: Subtract with 2 Regroupings

CA Standards
KEY NS 2.2, MR 1.2

Find $235 - 168$.

Step 1 Show the problem.

H	T	O
☐	☐	☐
2	3	5
1	6	8

Step 2 Regroup 1 ten as 10 ones.

H	T	O
☐	2	15
2	3̸	5̸
1	6	8
		7

Step 3 Regroup 1 hundred as 10 tens. Subtract.

H	T	O
1	12	15
2̸	3̸	5̸
1	6	8
	6	7

Solution: $235 - 168 = 67$

Subtract.

1. $\begin{array}{r} 622 \\ -433 \\ \hline \end{array}$

2. $\begin{array}{r} 254 \\ -169 \\ \hline \end{array}$

3. $\begin{array}{r} 147 \\ -93 \\ \hline \end{array}$

4. $\begin{array}{r} 324 \\ -248 \\ \hline \end{array}$

5. $\begin{array}{r} 526 \\ -437 \\ \hline \end{array}$

6. $\begin{array}{r} 355 \\ -268 \\ \hline \end{array}$

7. $\begin{array}{r} 742 \\ -355 \\ \hline \end{array}$

8. $\begin{array}{r} 621 \\ -222 \\ \hline \end{array}$

Spiral Review (Chapter 26, Lesson 1) **KEY** NS 2.2, MR 1.2

Subtract.

9. $\begin{array}{r} 7 \text{ hundreds} \\ -4 \text{ hundreds} \\ \hline \text{hundreds} \end{array}$ $\begin{array}{r} 700 \\ -400 \\ \hline \end{array}$

10. $\begin{array}{r} 8 \text{ hundreds} \\ -1 \text{ hundreds} \\ \hline \text{hundreds} \end{array}$ $\begin{array}{r} 800 \\ -100 \\ \hline \end{array}$

Use with text pp. 531–532

Hands On: Subtract with 2 Regroupings

CA Standards
KEY NS 2.2, MR 1.2

Solve.

1. Jen has 271 marbles. She gives 245 away to her friends. How many marbles does Jen have left?

    _____ marbles

2. Scott has collected 485 stamps. He loses 212 of them. How many stamps does Scott have left?

    _____ stamps

3. Carla counts 344 books at the library. Juan counts 167 books. How many more books does Carla count than Juan?

    _____ books

4. Tracy reads for 198 minutes. Her brother reads for 235 minutes. How many more minutes does Tracy's brother read than Tracy?

    _____ minutes

5. Todd takes a road trip. He drives 341 minutes for the first part of the trip. He takes a break for 45 minutes. Then he drives for 125 minutes for the second part of the trip. How much more time does Todd spend in the car on the first part of the trip than on the second part?

    _____ minutes

6. Jaclyn bought 342 pounds of pumpkins this year to carve. She also bought 812 candles. Last year, she bought 177 pounds of pumpkins. How many more pounds of pumpkins did Jaclyn buy this year than last year?

    _____ pounds

Subtract with 2 Regroupings

CA Standards
KEY NS 2.2, NS 2.0

Find 735 − 457.

6	12	15

$$
\begin{array}{c|c|c}
\cancel{7} & \cancel{3} & \cancel{5} \\
-4 & 5 & 7 \\
\hline
2 & 7 & 8
\end{array}
$$

Solution: 735 − 457 = 278

Subtract.

1. 855
   − 777

2. 362
   − 293

3. 475
   − 286

4. 325
   − 259

5. 792
   − 683

6. 727
   − 539

7. 192
   − 71

8. 364
   − 255

Spiral Review (Chapter 26, Lesson 2) **KEY** NS 2.2, MR 1.2

Use the ⬚, ▭, and ⬓.

Subtract.

9. 432
   − 216

10. 899
    − 547

11. 751
    − 635

Subtract with 2 Regroupings

Solve.

1. Joseph buys 421 ounces of water. His friend buys 632 ounces of water. How much more water does Joseph's friend buy than Joseph?

_____ ounces

2. Maria has a coin collection with 633 coins. She spends 122 coins. How many coins does Maria have left?

_____ coins

3. Helen counts 622 windows on the school building. Josh counts 499. How many more windows does Helen count than Josh?

_____ windows

4. Adam has 235 pebbles in his shoe. He removes 78 of them. How many pebbles does Adam still have left?

_____ pebbles

5. On Monday, Jessica read to page 137 in her book. The next day, she read to page 235. How many pages did Jessica read on Tuesday?

_____ pages

6. On Wednesday, 233 kids stayed home sick from school. In the middle of the day, 34 kids left school. On Thursday, 177 kids stayed home sick from school. How many more kids were sick at home on Wednesday than Thursday?

_____ kids

Name _____ Date _____

Subtract Across Zeros

CA Standards
KEY NS 2.2, NS 2.0

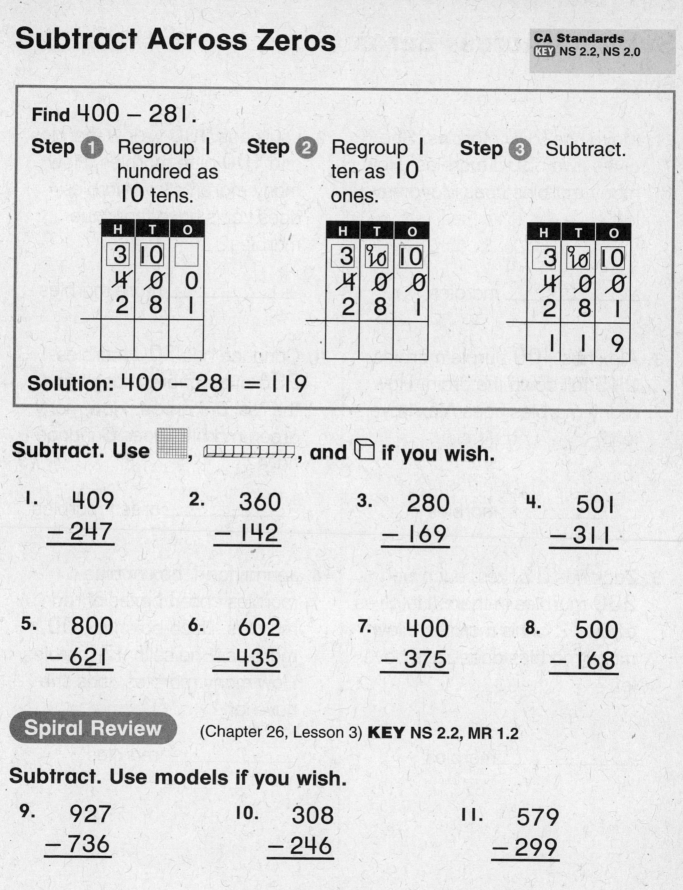

Find 400 − 281.

Step 1 Regroup 1 hundred as 10 tens.

H	T	O
3	10	
4̶	0̶	0
2	8	1

Step 2 Regroup 1 ten as 10 ones.

H	T	O
3	1̶0̶	10
4̶	0̶	0̶
2	8	1

Step 3 Subtract.

H	T	O
3	1̶0̶	10
4̶	0̶	0̶
2	8	1
1	1	9

Solution: 400 − 281 = 119

Subtract. Use ▦ , ▭▭▭▭ , and ▱ if you wish.

1. 409
   − 247

2. 360
   − 142

3. 280
   − 169

4. 501
   − 311

5. 800
   − 621

6. 602
   − 435

7. 400
   − 375

8. 500
   − 168

Spiral Review (Chapter 26, Lesson 3) **KEY NS 2.2, MR 1.2**

Subtract. Use models if you wish.

9. 927
   − 736

10. 308
   − 246

11. 579
   − 299

Use with text pp. 535–538

Subtract Across Zeros

Solve.

1. Maya has 900 marbles. She gives away 300 marbles. How many marbles does Maya have left?

   _____ marbles

2. Louis has 400 yellow marbles and 100 blue marbles. How many more yellow marbles does Louis have than blue marbles?

   _____ more marbles

3. Alex has 400 purple marbles. 245 fall down the drain. How many marbles does Alex have left?

   _____ marbles

4. Candace has 700 marbles. 236 of them are orange and the rest are green. How many green marbles does Candace have?

   _____ green marbles

5. Zack has 3 boxes, each with 200 marbles in them. He gives away 72 of his marbles. How many marbles does Zack have left?

   _____ marbles

6. Jenna has 1 box of blue marbles and 3 boxes of red marbles. Each box has 100 marbles. She sells 47 marbles. How many marbles does she have left?

   _____ marbles

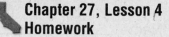
Write in Vertical Form

CA Standard
KEY NS 2.2

Find $257 + 621$.
First line up the ones.
Then line up the tens.
Add.

$$
\begin{array}{r}
2\ 5\ 7 \\
+\ 6\ 2\ 1 \\
\hline
8\ 7\ 8
\end{array}
$$

Solution: $257 + 621 = 878$

Add or subtract.

1. $721 + 232$ 2. $982 - 654$ 3. $754 - 629$ 4. $243 + 6$

_____ _____ _____ _____

5. $351 - 24$ 6. $810 + 76$ 7. $542 - 5$ 8. $289 + 102$

_____ _____ _____ _____

Spiral Review   (Chapter 26, Lesson 4) **KEY** NS 2.2

Subtract. Decide whether you need to regroup.

9.
$$
\begin{array}{r}
800 \\
-700 \\
\hline
\end{array}
$$

10.
$$
\begin{array}{r}
649 \\
-325 \\
\hline
\end{array}
$$

11.
$$
\begin{array}{r}
341 \\
-123 \\
\hline
\end{array}
$$

Write in Vertical Form

Write in vertical form to help solve.

1. Regina does homework for 25 minutes before dinner and 25 minutes after dinner. How long does Regina do homework for altogether?

_____ minutes

2. Josh has a bottle with 64 ounces of juice. He pours out 16 ounces to drink. How many ounces are left in the bottle?

_____ ounces

3. Adam reads 168 pages of a book on Monday and 37 pages on Tuesday. How many pages does Adam read altogether?

_____ pages

4. Jamal collects 235 American flag stamps and 182 rose stamps. How many more American flag stamps does Jamal collect?

_____ American flag stamps

5. Ellen walks for 47 minutes. She drives for 152 minutes. Then she walks another 56 minutes. How many minutes does Ellen walk?

_____ minutes

6. Shanika has 4 boxes of crayons. Each box has 100 crayons. 67 of the crayons break and are thrown away. How many crayons does Shanika have left?

_____ crayons

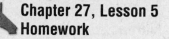
Write a Number Sentence

CA Standard
KEY NS 2.2

The second grade went to the Science Museum.

They spent 40 minutes at the space show.

Then they went to the exhibits for 90 minutes.

How many minutes did the second grade

spend at the museum altogether?

Write an number sentence.

Then solve.

__40__ (+) __90__ = __130__ minutes

Write a number sentence. Then solve.

1. The bus took 65 minutes to get to the museum and 40 minutes to return to school. How many minutes was the class on the bus?

   __65__ ◯ __40__ = _____

   minutes

2. How many more minutes did they spend at the exhibit than at the show?

   __90__ ◯ __40__ = _____

   minutes

Spiral Review   (Chapter 26, Lesson 5)   **KEY** NS 2.2, MR 2.0

Write a number sentence. Then solve.

3. Janna counts 417 fish at the aquarium. Greg counts 269. How many more fish does Janna count?

   _____ _____ = _____ fish

Name _____ Date _____

Write a Number Sentence

Mrs. Hudson's class has a read-a-thon. The table shows some of their results.

Name	Number of Pages Read
Sue	392
Pedro	531
Candace	218
Nathaniel	647

Use the table and write a number sentence to solve the problem.

1. Who read the most pages?

   _____

2. Which student read the least number of pages?

   _____

3. How many more pages did Pedro read than Candace?

   ____ ◯ ____ ◯ ____
   pages

4. How many more pages did Nathaniel read than Sue?

   ____ ◯ ____ ◯ ____
   pages

5. How many more pages did Sue and Pedro read together than Candace and Nathaniel read together?

   ____ ◯ ____ ◯ ____ ◯ ____ ◯ ____
   pages

6. Candace forgot to mark down 100 pages that she read. How many more pages does Sue read than Candace?

   ____ ◯ ____ ◯ ____ ◯ ____ pages

Hands On: Add and Subtract Money

CA Standards
KEY NS 5.1, KEY NS 5.2

You can use bills and coins to help add and subtract money.
Model the amounts with coins and bills. Add or subtract.
Regroup 100 cents as a dollar if you can.

To add:

$4.07
+$379
$7.86

To subtract:

$3.18
−$1.85
$1.33

Write the sum or difference.

1. $6.11
    −$4.56

2. $2.54
    +$1.66

3. $1.47
    −$0.99

4. $4.24
    +$2.11

5. $5.99
    −$2.48

6. $3.00
    +$2.98

7. $7.62
    −$3.55

8. $1.81
    +$2.22

Spiral Review (Chapter 27, Lesson 1) **KEY NS 2.2, MR 1.2**

Subtract.

9.   822
    −633

10. 212
    −189

11. 158
    −99

12. 148
    −69

Hands On: Add and Subtract Money

Solve.

1. Cory buys a red ball for $2.00 and a blue ball for $3.00. How much money does Cory spend?

   $_____

2. Jason buys a toy racecar for $4.00 and a toy truck for $1.00. How much money does Jason spend?

   $_____

3. Shirley buys a book for $2.75. She pays with a $5 bill. How much change does Shirley get back?

   $_____

4. A steam boat costs $6.75. A canoe costs $4.25. How much more does the steam boat cost than the canoe?

   $_____

5. Tracy buys some socks for $2.57. She also buys a pair of shoes for $7.00. She pays with a $10 bill. How much change does Tracy get in return?

   _____

6. Adam buys two books for $4.75 each. He pays with a $10 bill. How much change should Adam receive?

   _____

Add and Subtract Money

CA Standard
KEY NS 5.2

Use a dollar sign and a decimal point
when you add and subtract money.

Find $2.25 + $0.45.

$2.25
+0.45
_____
$2.70

Find $4.21 − $2.89.

3 11 11
$4.21
−2.89
_____
$1.32

Add or Subtract.

1. $1.22
   +3.18

2. $0.50
   +4.50

3. $5.75
   −2.51

4. $9.00
   −0.08

**Write the number sentence in vertical form.
Then add or subtract.**

5. $4.01 − $0.29

6. $1.56 + $2.16

_____   _____

Spiral Review   (Chapter 27, Lesson 2) **KEY** NS 2.2, NS 2.0

Subtract.

7.   455
    −355

8.   623
    −439

9.   431
    −286

10. 543
    −259

Add and Subtract Money

CA Standard
KEY NS 5.2

Use the Lunch Menu to solve the problems.

Lunch Menu	
Items	**Cost**
Ham Sandwich	$3.82
Tuna Sandwich	$4.15
Cheese Sandwich	$2.45
Fruit Juice	$1.32
Milk	$0.95

1. What costs more, a ham sandwich or a cheese sandwich?

_____

2. Does a fruit juice or a milk cost less?

_____

3. Raymond buys a tuna sandwich. Gloria buys a cheese sandwich. How much money do they spend in all?

_____

4. Tamara buys a ham sandwich and one milk. How much does she spend?

_____

5. Enrique buys a ham sandwich and fruit juice. He pays with a $10 bill. How much change should he get?

_____

6. Alee buys a ham sandwich. Then she buys a cheese sandwich for her brother. She pays with a $10 bill. How much change should she get?

_____

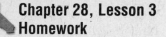
Check Subtraction

CA Standard
KEY NS 2.1

Addition can be used to check subtraction.
The sum should equal the number you
subtracted from.

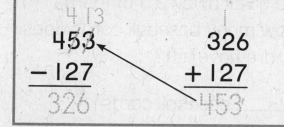

$$
\begin{array}{r} 4\ \ 13 \\ 453 \\ -127 \\ \hline 326 \end{array}
\qquad
\begin{array}{r} 326 \\ +127 \\ \hline 453 \end{array}
$$

Subtract.
Check by adding.

1. $\begin{array}{r} 362 \\ -155 \\ \hline \end{array}$ +

2. $\begin{array}{r} 449 \\ -228 \\ \hline \end{array}$ +

3. $\begin{array}{r} 575 \\ -249 \\ \hline \end{array}$ +

4. $\begin{array}{r} 166 \\ -\ \ 86 \\ \hline \end{array}$ +

Spiral Review   (Chapter 27, Lesson 3) **KEY** NS 2.2, NS 2.0

Subtract. Use ▦ , ▭ , **and** ◻ **if you wish.**

5. $\begin{array}{r} 603 \\ -421 \\ \hline \end{array}$

6. $\begin{array}{r} 890 \\ -682 \\ \hline \end{array}$

7. $\begin{array}{r} 500 \\ -\ 37 \\ \hline \end{array}$

8. $\begin{array}{r} 100 \\ -\ 68 \\ \hline \end{array}$

Use with text pp. 555–556

Check Subtraction

CA Standard
KEY NS 2.1

Subtract to solve. Check by adding.

1. Karla brings 15 apples to school. She gives away 9. How many apples does Karla have left?

_____ apples

2. André has 32 baseball cards. He gives away 23 of them. How many baseball cards does André have left?

_____ baseball cards

3. The craft club makes 382 candles. They sell 218 candles at the fair. How many candles do they have left?

_____ candles

4. There are 145 tiles in the box. Yoshi uses 92 of the tiles. How many tiles are left in the box?

_____ tiles

5. A theater has 985 tickets for a play. There are 1,000 seats in the theater. The ticket office sells 678 tickets. How many tickets are left?

_____ tickets

6. Yesterday Lori completed a puzzle with 500 pieces. Today she is working on a puzzle with 750 pieces. She connects 126 pieces of the puzzle. How many pieces of the puzzle are left?

_____ pieces

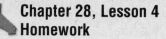
Estimate Sums and Differences

CA Standards
NS 6.0, NS 2.0

Find the nearest hundred for each number in the problem.
Then add.

480   nearest hundred   →   500
+310 nearest hundred   → + 300
                              800

Solution: The sum of 480 and 310 is about ___800___.

Find the nearest hundred. Add or subtract.

1.   120
   +360   + ____

2.   410
   −280   − ____

3.   690
   +115   + ____

4.   927
   −568   − ____

Spiral Review (Chapter 27, Lesson 4) **KEY** NS 2.2

Write in vertical form. Add or subtract.

5. 681 + 235

6. 724 − 187

7. 502 + 397

   + ____

   − ____

   + ____

Use with text pp. 557–558

Estimate Sums and Differences

CA Standards
NS 6.0, NS 2.0

**Round the numbers to the nearest hundred
to solve.**

1. Caitlin drives 400 miles on Saturday. On Sunday she drives 200 miles. How many miles does Caitlin drive in all?

_____ miles

2. Peter reads for 600 minutes on Monday. On Tuesday he reads for 100 minutes. How many minutes does Peter read on Monday and Tuesday combined?

_____ minutes

3. Ariel has 580 beads. She gives away 230 of them. How many beads does Ariel have left?

_____ ◯ _____ ◯ _____

beads

4. Andrew reads 280 pages of his book. Cecile reads 480 pages of her book. How many more pages does Cecile read than Andrew?

_____ ◯ _____ ◯ _____

pages

5. Donna hikes for 430 minutes before lunch. She eats lunch for 120 minutes. She hikes for 370 minutes after lunch. How many minutes does Donna hike in all?

_____ ◯ _____ ◯ _____

minutes

6. Ryan runs for 120 minutes. He stops for a rest for 50 minutes and then he runs for another 240 minutes. How many minutes does Ryan run in all?

_____ ◯ _____ ◯ _____

minutes

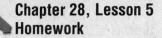
Work Backward

CA Standards
KEY NS 2.1, AF 1.2

Work backward to solve the problem.

Mr. Harris took his class to the planetarium. He took 27 students in all.
12 of the students were girls. How many boys did Mr. Harris take?

First write a number sentence with the information you know.

boys + girls = all students

____?____ + ☐12☐ = ____27____

Then work backward and find the missing part by subtracting.

__27__ − __12__ = __15__

Mr. Harris took 15 boys.

Work backward to solve the problem.

1. Anita buys 65 pens. 37 of the pens are black. The rest of the pens
   are blue. How many blue pens does Anita buy?

   _____ blue pens

2. Janet has 57 buttons in her button jar. 34 of the buttons are round.
   How many of the buttons are not round?

   _____ buttons

Spiral Review   (Chapter 27, Lesson 5) **AF 1.3, KEY NS 2.2, SDAP 1.4**

Write a number sentence to solve the problem.

3. Jay has 27 stickers. Beth has 102 stickers. How many
   stickers do they have together?

   _____

Homework
285
Use with text pp. 559–562

Problem Solving: Work Backward

CA Standards
KEY NS 2.1, AF 1.2

Work backward to solve the problems.

1. Candace has 46 students in her class. 23 of the students are girls. How many students are boys? (Hint: Work backward and subtract the number of girls from the total number.)

_____ boys

2. James goes to his friend's birthday party. There are 23 people at the party. 11 are girls. How many boys are at the party? (Hint: Subtract the number of girls from the total number of people.)

_____ boys

3. Emily is reading a book with 425 pages. She has read 235 pages. How many more pages does Emily have left to read?

_____ pages

4. Joe is reading a book with 567 pages. He has read 347 pages already. How many pages does Joe have left to read?

_____ pages

5. Hilary has a collection of 582 marbles. 324 marbles are red and 102 marbles are blue. The rest of the marbles are green. How many green marbles does Hilary have?

_____ green marbles

6. Rob has a collection of 718 marbles. 479 of the marbles are purple and 112 of the marbles are yellow. The rest of the marbles are orange. How many orange marbles does Rob have?

_____ orange marbles

Use with text pp. 559–562